TAKE FIVE

TAKE FIVE

· · · · · · · · · · · · · · · · · · ·

Devotions

to Strengthen

a Man's

Relationships

· · · · · · · · · · · · · · · · · · ·

EDITED BY **ROBERT BUSHA**

BROADMAN
& HOLMAN
PUBLISHERS

Nashville, Tennessee

Printed in the United States of America

4253-67
0-8054-5367-9

Dewey Decimal Classification: 242.642
Subject Heading: DEVOTIONAL LITERATURE // MEN—RELIGIOUS LIFE
Library of Congress Card Catalog Number: 93-45613

Library of Congress Cataloging-in-Publication Data
Take five! : devotions to strengthen a man's relationships / Robert
Busha, editor.
    p. cm.
    ISBN 0-8054-5367-9
    1. Men—Prayer-books and devotions—English.   2. Interpersonal
relations—Religious aspects—Christianity.   3. Christian life—1960–
I. Busha, Robert, 1943– .
BV4843.T356   1994
242'.642—dc20   93-45613
                                                                            CIP

*This volume of Take Five is dedicated to my soul mate,
kindred spirit, and wife, Mary Catherine.
God has blessed me with immense love and support
from this special partner and with the remarkable personal,
professional, and spiritual affinity we share.
Each and every day she makes it possible for me
to be far better than I have ever been.*

Acknowledgments

Thanks to the staff at Broadman & Holman Publishers, especially our editor, Janis Whipple, for the opportunity to share; and to my wife, Mary Catherine, my collaborator, editor, and continuing source for support and encouragement.

Contents

Introduction: Memorable Victories

Following our Saturday afternoon workout on the tennis court, Kent and I wandered over to the third base side of a nearby baseball field to watch a little league game. At the plate was a boy of about ten who appeared to be bigger around than he was tall. Many spectators affectionately used the name "Tubby" as they shouted encouragement from the sidelines.

We heard the umpire remind everyone of the three-two count, with two out. The scoreboard clearly indicated the team in the field was way ahead. So, for practical purposes, no matter what he did, Tubby wasn't going to change the outcome of the game. But, with the next pitch, a very fundamental change did occur in the way the game ended.

The ball left the pitcher's hand and came in straight down the middle. Tubby's bat came around and connected. The ball arched high into right field. About the same moment the ball landed in the right fielder's glove, ending the game, Tubby crossed first base, accompanied by "atta-boy" and cheering from his team, his coaches, and wild, happy family members in the grandstands. As they clapped and shouted, many of the spectators rushed to congratulate Tubby. The air was filled with sounds of celebration and warm feelings.

As late observers, Kent and I were momentarily confused. Tubby was out. His team lost. Why were they all so happy?

We soon learned that during the entire season, which included many games and practice sessions, not one time had he even fouled it off. Not once! This was the very first time Tubby had ever hit the ball.

So this simple act of connecting bat to ball was a victory of sorts. And the spontaneous celebration of that event by his coaches, teammates, and their families was an act of very thoughtful and deliberate love much more important than wins and losses, or trophies and championships.

I'm absolutely sure that event was important to Tubby, one of the most important in his life. The memory of that sweet moment must certainly have been an inspiration to him on other occasions. It was important to me, too.

No matter how slow or halting my progress as a Christian, I know the coaching I get from Him will be thoughtful and patient, and I can count on the loving support and encouragement from the huge crowd of faithful believers in His grandstands.

Take a few minutes and think about Tubby and the relationships around him. Think about yours as well while reading the devotions in this volume of *Take Five*. The various pains, pleasures, and insights of the Christian men who are sharing their experiences will, I'm sure, be just as inspiring as Tubby's memorable victory.

Father,

thanks for Your loving patience as I work through the game plan You have for me. You know I need all the coaching I can get as I work toward victory.

Amen.

Robert Busha

For the anxious longing of the creation
waits eagerly for the revealing of the sons of God ...
that the creation...will be set free.

Romans 8:19–21, NASB

My Son Left Home Today

Gene Wilder

Today my son left home alone. I faced his departure with mixed emotions. He faced the day with everything to gain. I faced the day with much to lose.

Sixteen years old. To him, the age meant freedom. To me, the age declared the beginning of a new relationship. Life would never be the same again. I knew it. He knew it. He was thrilled. I struggled.

Yes, today my son left home alone. He'd never done that before. In the past, someone always left with him. Before today someone was there to watch out for him. But today he left home alone, and I found it hard to hold back the tears.

Now, don't misunderstand me. I trust my son. It's the rest of the world I don't trust. Others don't love him as I do. To me, he's the most important sixteen-year-old in the world. To others, he's just another crazy teenager.

Today my son left home alone, experiencing the freedom of his new driver's license. I didn't have to let him go. I could have refused, but I didn't. Instead, I celebrated his new freedom with him. Little does he know that when he left, he took a big piece of my heart with him.

How strange. Because I loved him, I didn't want to let him go. But because I loved him, I celebrated his freedom with him. Love and logic are, indeed, strange bedfellows.

Today, I also learned something new about my heavenly Father. Like all fathers, He surely must have struggled with the urge to restrict my freedom and maintain protective control over my life, but He didn't. Instead, He celebrated my right to choose, even at the risk of my being wrong sometimes.

As I walk through life on my own, however, I sense a new dimension to my freedom. I never walk alone. For somewhere deep inside this son, my Father has left a big piece of His heart.

Dear Lord,
thank You for the freedom of Your love.
As I travel down the highway of life,
help me to heed the voice within.
In Jesus' name I pray.
Amen.

There is no fear in love.
But perfect love drives out fear.

1 John 4:18, NIV

Perfect Love

Don M. Aycock

My wife, Carla, and I have been married twenty years. We're the very proud parents of twin boys, Ryan and Christopher, who are twelve at this writing.

When I reflect on our lives together I wonder how I could ever refer to any of what we've experienced as planned, logical, or ordinary. Yet in its own way this is exactly what our life together has been.

Our story is unique in some of its details, but many, many people have had similar experiences in coming to love. People who didn't even like each other at first, later ended up happily hitched, completely in love.

We've come to understand that love is not some abstract, bloodless, lifeless principle. Love is both mysterious and marvelous. I've experienced healing and nearly indescribable support in my marriage.

The love between a man and woman in marriage is as much the work of God as is His love for mankind. Both are theologically oriented. That's why a church is the proper place for weddings, if at all possible. The building itself—its decorations and surroundings—says symbolically,

"There is a third party involved in this union." The same One who said, "Let there be light," also said, "Let there be love."

The apostle John is right. There is no fear in love. Our homes are to be a refuge from the chaos and fear of this world. That's a fact that pushes us to give our best to our homes. It also leads us to thank God for them.

Thank You, Lord,
for giving me a home where love lives.
It may not be a perfect place,
but it's mine and I promise to give You my best effort
to build and protect it, to make it a source of perfect love.
Let Your love cast out all fear there.
Amen.

Is This a Big One?

Harold J. Behm

"Dad, is this a big one or a medium?" I asked as I helped my father sort apples in the shade of the big maple tree in our front yard, which was the sales area for the Winding Trail Farm orchards. In the fall, the yard was filled with baskets of apples of many varieties: Jonathan, Grimes Golden, Red Delicious, Yellow Delicious, Wealthy, York Imperial, to name a few.

To maintain quality, Dad always sorted baskets of apples before placing them for sale in the yard. And so he would dump several bushels of apples on the grass for sorting.

As a young boy I always wanted to be in on everything, but sorting applies by eye required judgment. Often, what looked like a big apple to me was only a medium-sized one according to Dad.

So Dad got the idea of drilling different sized holes in a board to standardize the sorting for me. Those apples too big for the largest hole were "large" apples. "Mediums" were ones that went through the largest hole but not the next to the largest hole. Any that went through the smallest hole were called culls and were fed to the hogs.

Testing every apple against the board slowed the sorting process considerably. I soon learned to use the board only as a standard—to set my eye, so to speak. Only occasionally did I need to test an apple on the board to be sure that my eye was still "in calibration."

It has been many years since I helped sort apples on the Winding Trail Farm, but I still remember guidelines my father set, not just for sorting apples, but in many other areas of life as well—reliable, unchanging standards.

Lord,

I pray that all young boys could have the benefit of a father

who cares enough to set standards and guidelines for their lives.

Thank You for those set forth in Your Word.

Amen.

Above all,
love each other deeply.

1 Peter 4:8, NIV

I Love You, Dad

Charles R. Brown

Night traffic on the road to Los Angeles was bearable. The old Dodge van pushed hard to keep up with the more experienced freeway racers.

For several miles my dad and I stared into the darkness. We didn't say much. We'd never said much to each other over the years. Words that were exchanged were forced. I was glad I was driving. It gave me an excuse not to look him in the face. Why was it so hard to look my dad in the face?

We were on our way to an appointment with a chaplain at the Union Rescue Mission. Dad had finally agreed to seek help in his battle with drinking.

Bits and pieces of my father's history grudgingly came from his sixty-three-year-old mouth. Expressions of disappointment, frustration, and failure pierced the air. My stomach was in knots as I listened.

Then I glanced at him briefly, purposely looked at him eye-to-eye, and said, "I love you, Dad." And suddenly the invisible barrier between us, built up by years of silence, melted away.

As we neared our destination I was struck by a nerve-shaking thought. Here I was, at age thirty-two, and I couldn't remember the last time I'd looked Dad squarely in the face and told him I loved him.

About eleven years later Dad quietly slipped into the other side of this life. I'm so grateful I had the opportunity to say those words frequently to him during those last few years. As I wrote to him and phoned him and visited with him, I made an extra effort to tell him that I loved and cared for him.

Four little words packed with so much power, yet for far too long those same four words had been deliberately choked in our throats.

I have since made it a point to encourage my children to *word* their relationships with people—especially family. The hope I've expressed to them is that they'd never get too old nor too big to give their parents a hug or express words of affection.

Recently my twenty-two-year-old son drove me to a store and just out of the blue he glanced over at me and said, "I love you." This dad's uninhibited response? "I love you, too, son. Thanks for going to the store with me."

Lord,

thank You for my dad.

Thank You for the time to get to know him better.

Thank You, Father, for first saying to me,

"I love you, son."

Amen.

Nevertheless I am continually with Thee;
Thou hast taken hold of my right hand.

Psalm 73:23, NASB

Men at Prayer

John B. Calsin, Jr.

Due to circumstances in today's American society, a Christian man may feel reluctant to hold another man's hand.

In my church it's not uncommon for the congregation to join hands in prayer. In spite of that, I sometimes feel it's not manly as I join with other men when they link their hands together.

One morning, as I entered the church early to pray, I was cold, due to the chill in the air. A number of the men were already gathered in a circle, near the altar rail, holding hands and praying for the needs of others. As I walked up to join the group, my reluctance once again became apparent to me.

Two men in the circle dropped their grip and stepped aside so I could join in the supplications. Their hands were warm and mine were cold. Soon I began to physically warm up. Beyond that, however, something spiritually warmed in me as well.

As the psalm writer observed, he was always with God and God held him. While my fellow churchmen stood in their circle, holding hands and praying, I knew somehow we were holding the hand of God, too. My discomfort lessened and, together, we touched Him for the needs of others.

Lord,
as You hold my hand,
help me to hold the hands of others
both in prayer and during the struggles
they experience in their lives.
Amen.

Whatever you did
for one of the least of these brothers of mine,
you did for me.

Matthew 25:40, NIV

See the Person, See Christ

Jerry Cook

Some time ago I met a young man who was saved from the streets of one of our major cities. He had lived there since he was eleven years old—when he was first introduced into child prostitution by a man who ran a string of boys in the downtown district.

When this young man was seventeen, a street preacher befriended him and ultimately led him to Christ. I asked him what he found to be the hardest part of living on the street. I knew he had been cold and hungry, had slept under bridges, and had endured the many ordeals that homeless people face. I thought he would speak of the loneliness or cold or danger—any number of things came to mind.

He didn't mention any of those things, however. Instead he said, "The hardest part of living on the street was that nobody ever looked at me. People would always pretend that I didn't exist. When they would walk by, they'd always look the other way, and I felt like they wished I was dead, and then I began to wish I was dead, because I really wasn't anybody."

Do you know what the man who led him to Christ did? He simply looked at him and said, "Young man, you look kind of lonely. Would you like to talk?" That broke him up. He told me, "Other people, if they looked at all, would quickly glance away. But I was a person to him. I mattered. And because I mattered to him, I could begin to believe that I might matter to God, if one existed."

As I listened to that young man, I thought of the times I too had averted my eyes from people who were not particularly comfortable to look at, for whatever reason. True, there may have been humane and proper reasons to avert my eyes sometimes. More often than not, however, it was just what the street boy knew it to be—a refusal to recognize someone as a person. It is easy to look past people and never really see them. I've also learned that you can look at people and still not see them.

I have never lived on the streets as the young man no one would look at. I have never been abandoned and rejected. I have, however, experienced the sense of isolation that comes from being looked at but not seen by those around me.

Dear Lord,
take my life and use it to bring life in You to others,
especially those lost souls whose eyes are avoided,
whose hearts may appear to be beyond touch,
and whose souls may seem beyond salvation.
Allow me to recognize that You are the only judge of that reckoning.
May I be Your instrument.
Amen.

If possible, so far as it depends on you, be at peace with all men.

Romans 12:18, NASB

If Possible, Make Peace

Jack Cunningham

"Don't talk to me," my friend snapped.

"But, Julie,"

"Get away, Jack."

I trudged off, with a heavy heart and sick soul. I'd only wanted to make things right with her, but she wouldn't listen. For weeks I'd struggled with compounded guilt. First, I'd offended her, and what I'd done was tearing out my insides. Second, despite my numerous attempts, I couldn't make peace with her, so I felt like I was displeasing Christ, too. It was as if a Damoclean sword was about to snuff out my life—my spiritual life—for good. I couldn't continue serving God with this torment.

Then one afternoon as I arrived home from work Romans 12:18 hit me. The short phrase "if possible" leapt into my thoughts. I had tried to make peace with Julie. Indeed, I'd done everything I knew to do, but it simply wasn't possible. So why was I feeling guilty? I'd done all that God required of me. There was nothing else I could do. With this realization burning in my heart, my guilt suddenly vanished. The next move belonged to her. I slept soundly for the first night in a long time.

Sadly, Julie never forgave me. And I learned that we can't always repair a broken fellowship, although this shouldn't stop us from trying. All God asks is that we attempt to make peace with those whom we've offended. Once we do this, guilty feelings no longer have a place in our hearts, for we've obeyed God.

Dear Lord,

thank You for teaching me to be a peacemaker

and for delivering me from all feelings of guilt

when my attempts at peacemaking fail.

In Jesus' name.

Amen.

For over all the glory
there will be a covering.

Isaiah 4:5, NKJV

Overcover Agents

Dean Davis

If ever my son asks me to define, in a single word, the essence of manhood, I think I'll be ready. I'll take him to the Book of Isaiah, read him this enigmatic prophecy of the kingdom of God, and underline the one crucial word: *covering*.

I must explain that I didn't learn the lesson reading Isaiah. I learned it when an unexpected providence made me manager of a local Christian bookstore. Suddenly, a callow young man with neither business nor administrative experience found himself responsible not only for the smooth and profitable operation of a thriving store, but also for the guidance and safety of several other dedicated employees—all of whom happened to be ladies!

Looking back, it seems to me that somehow, in my day-to-day relationship with these women, God quietly, but unalterably, granted me a revelation of manhood: to be a man was to stand for the Father in His world, and to cover—that is, to protect and provide for—the creatures He entrusts to our care, especially women and children.

The revelation came, I'm sure, in the little things: figuring out how to schedule lunches or days off so the ladies wouldn't get tired nor miss events that were important to them; sending them home sick, even when they wanted to stay; lifting heavy boxes from their arms; stepping in between them and difficult customers; even coaxing the owner to give them raises!

And what was the payoff in all these little chivalries? Beyond the love and respect of my staff, it was simply this: I experienced my manhood. Why? Because I experienced my God covering these women through me, His man. Having granted a small stewardship of His authority and loving oversight, He fulfilled me as a man.

If we are Christians, the kingdom that Isaiah foresaw is here, though we indeed groan till it appears in fullness. Therefore, over all our assemblies—our personal walk with Christ, our home, our place of work, our church, our chosen sphere of service in the community—a glory should be seen, an orderliness, an integrity, a holy joy.

But it can only be seen if there is a covering over the glory. And there can only be a covering if God can gather His men to Himself.

Father,

You know how difficult it is for me to be a man,

to lead when I would rather follow, fight when I would rather run.

In a world where so many of Your children

are abandoned by the men in their lives, help me to become an

"overcover agent."

Help me more and more to provide and protect—

to cover the needy whom You are pleased to entrust to my care.

In His name, who showed me the way.

Amen.

Yet I am always with you; you hold me by my right hand.
You guide me with your counsel, and afterward you will take me
into glory. Whom have I in heaven but you? And being with You,
I desire nothing on earth. My flesh and my heart may fail,
but God is the strength of my heart and my portion forever.

Psalm 73:23–26, NIV

His Encompassing Love

James Dobson

On August 15, 1990, I was playing an early morning round of basketball. At fifty-four years of age, I thought I was in great physical condition. I had recently undergone a medical examination and was pronounced to be in excellent health. I could play basketball all day with men twenty-five years my junior.

Suddenly, I was stricken by a moderate pain in the center of my chest. I excused myself, telling my friends I didn't feel well. Then I foolishly drove alone to a nearby emergency clinic and booked a room.

Hospital staff came at me from every direction. Tubes and IVs were strung all over me. An automatic blood pressure machine pumped frantically on my arm every five minutes throughout the night, and a nurse delicately suggested that I not move unless absolutely necessary. That does tend to get your attention. As I lay there in the darkness listening to the *beep-beep-beep* of the oscilloscope, I began to think very clearly about the people I loved and what things did and did not really matter.

During those last nine days in the cardiac care unit, I was keenly aware of the implications of my illness. There was one brief period, however, when my confidence began to crumble. The day before I was discharged, I underwent an angiogram to determine the nature of my arterial network and the extent of my heart damage. The initial report from that procedure was much more threatening than would later be confirmed, and those ominous findings did not escape my notice.

For the first time in the long ordeal, anxiety swept over me. That's when I uttered a brief and ineloquent prayer from the depths of my soul. I said, "Lord, you know where I am right now. And you know that I am upset and very lonely. Would you send someone who can help me?"

A short time later, my good friend Dr. Jack Hayford unexpectedly walked through the door. We greeted each other warmly, and then I said, "Jack, why did you take the time to come see me today?" I didn't tell him about my prayer.

He said, "Because the Lord told me you were lonely."

That's the kind of God we serve. Now admittedly, the Lord doesn't always solve our problems instantaneously, and He sometimes permits us to walk through the valley of the shadow of death. But He is there with us even in the darkest hours, and we can never escape His encompassing love. I was warmly embraced by it throughout my hospitalization, even in the darkest hour.

Father God,

You know when I need Your hand, Your touch of reassurance.

In my darkest hours You send comforters,

and I'm reminded of Your unbounded loved for me.

Thank You, Father.

Amen.

Be wise in the way you act toward outsiders;
make the most of every opportunity.

Colossians 4:5, NIV

Being Ready Always

Phil Downer

When God brings opportunities to serve Him, He doesn't ask whether the timing is convenient for us. I learned this lesson the hard way, returning home from Washington, D.C., after a week filled with legal depositions and courtroom appearances. Tired and wanting to do nothing more than unwind, I hardly noticed the man seated next to me on the plane. A nap, not conversation, was what I wanted.

As the jet's wheels thudded on the Atlanta runway, I reached for my litigation case under the seat in front of me.

"Phil Downer!" the man next to me exclaimed, seeing the name tag. To my surprise, he was my big brother from my fraternity days in college. We sat together for ninety-five minutes, but I hadn't said a word to him.

Immediately I wondered how my old friend was doing spiritually, but there was not time to find out. He was eager to get home, and after an exchange of pleasantries, we parted ways. A missed opportunity! God had arranged an appointment for me with an old friend, and I had slept through it.

Since then, I have called him several times. We have talked briefly, but there has not been a second chance to meet so I could tell him about the great things the Lord has been doing in my life since those crazy college days.

Several years later, I was again on a plane, en route to a conference. I was engrossed in the week's assignment for a couples' Bible study my wife, Susy, and I were involved in. Halfway through the flight, it occurred to me that I had not said anything to the young boy sitting next to me. Wondering if he knew the Lord, I started talking with him.

Over the next minutes, I learned that his parents were going through a messy divorce. Some of his hurts reminded me of my own difficult childhood. As we talked, I explained how God enabled me to overcome similar pain after I asked Jesus to come into my life. Using a helpful little booklet I always carry, I showed how we are separated from God by sin and that Christ is the only way to bridge this separation.

This twelve-year-old boy listened intently. After a few minutes, he bowed his head with me to ask the Lord Jesus into his life. What a joy it was to be God's agent in introducing this young fellow to the best news in life! And to think I almost missed another divine opportunity because I was preoccupied with a Bible study when God was calling me to be a living Bible in the life of another individual.

Heavenly Father,
I am so easily distracted.
Help me to remain sensitive to Your leading and open to
opportunities You send my way—even when they aren't convenient.
Thank You for those who took the time to tell me about You.
May I be ready always to pass this Good News on to others.
Amen.

Who desires everyone to be saved
and to come to the knowledge of the truth.

1 Timothy 2:4, RSV

Taking the Time

Bernard Epperson

For two years I worked in a youth ministry at an inner city park. We went there every Saturday during the summer, where we set up a large sound system, and talked to the teens. In the evening we set up a huge plywood screen, showed an evangelistic film, and gave an altar call.

We were doing well and the teens were turning to the Lord. We prayed with each one, passed out Bibles, and tried to hook them up with churches in the community. It was a good work, and it kept us very busy.

One afternoon an old man came into the park. He seemed to hang around, as if he wanted to talk. As I worked with the teens he stuck in my mind. The Lord seemed to be asking me to take a few minutes and talk to him. The teens went to play basketball, and I went to introduce myself to the old man.

He was glad to meet me, and he did want to talk. He lived near the park and had noticed our work. I asked if he'd ever been saved, and he said he thought so, but it was many years ago. I prayed with him again and then gave him a Bible. Tears came to his eyes, and he promised to start going back to church. He thanked me for my time and then left, and I returned to the teens.

In the next couple of weeks the old man came through the park often and said hello to me. I always took a moment to ask how he was doing.

Nearly a month after I prayed with him, some of the teens told me the old man had died. I was glad that I had taken the time to leave what I was doing for that few minutes to talk and pray with him. God had surely directed this meeting, and I know He's glad for each person that comes into His kingdom.

Lord,

You always take time for me.

Help me to always take time to pray

and encourage each person I can to come to You.

Amen.

So if there is any encouragement in Christ, any incentive of love,
any participation in the Spirit, any affection and sympathy,
complete my joy by being of the same mind, having the same love,
being in full accord and of one mind.

Philemon 2:1–2, RSV

How Many Chances Have I Blown?

Mark L. Evans

As the sports editor of a small-town daily newspaper, I come in regular contact with a lot of high school athletes. Many of them become my friends. One young woman, who was an outstanding basketball player and a very talented artist, was such a friend.

This young lady was one of the players who always took time to speak to me after games. She was somewhat quiet, but certainly not shy, and attractive as well as talented. When she accepted a basketball scholarship to attend a small Christian college about one hundred miles away from home, I was delighted for her. My delight turned to horror at the end of her freshman year when I heard the tragic news about her.

This nineteen-year-old woman, apparently having flunked part of her finals, had killed herself. Later I learned more details. Apparently she had driven part of the way home and had pulled off the road and shot herself. It was only after I heard those details that a scary thought struck me: Had she left campus still undecided about whether or not to take her own life?

This thought, of course, brings up an even more troubling question. If she had not yet decided when she left campus, how many Christian friends and acquaintances did she cross paths with during this time of crisis and indecision?

Upon further meditation, I had to stop and ask myself a difficult question. Have I unknowingly encountered anyone in such a desperate state? It horrifies me to think that I could be having a bad day or be distracted by some comparatively minor problem and snap at, or brush away, someone in the throes of a life-and-death struggle just as this troubled young woman experienced.

Teenage suicide, in particular, is becoming a major problem in America. Of course, depression and hopelessness that can lead to suicide are certainly not restricted to adolescents. The tragic loss of this talented young woman definitely made me stop and think. How may I be of help to someone considering a final solution to a temporary problem?

Lord Jesus,

please grant me the discernment to feel the hurt of those around me
and to know when and especially how to reach out to them.
Please place me in such situations and help me to have the incentive
of love and participation in the Spirit to help these people.
In Jesus' name I pray.
Amen.

Speak out for those who cannot speak,
for the rights of all the destitute.
Speak out...defend the rights of the poor.

Proverbs 31:8–9, NRSV

Speak Out for Others

William H. Gentz

One of the blessings of my childhood was having a deaf-mute playmate. I learned early in life that there are fellow human beings who need others to speak for them.

From our playmate we learned the rudiments of the sign language so we could use our voices to make his needs known to others. Recently the drama and film *Children of a Lesser God* made this desperate need real to me again.

The message from Proverbs gives a much wider application of this need to "speak for those who cannot speak." God calls us to look around and see others with this same need. For example, little children caught in the webs of poverty, crime, parental abuse, and drugs need the voices of those of us who can speak about their plight to authorities at all levels of society and government.

Many other disenfranchised persons in our society today fit into the word the Bible uses here, "the destitute." The homeless, the handicapped, the forsaken in our country need others to speak for them, to defend their cause, and to claim their rights. And if we raise our sights to the millions who are hungry in the world, the victims of war, famine, disaster, and persecution in other countries, the needs become almost overwhelming.

Each of us can make a difference in our community, our nation, and our world through participation in relief efforts through our churches and charities. Together we can feed the hungry, comfort the needy, and heal the sick. Over and above that broad objective, however, in response to God's call we can also "speak for those who cannot speak." The need has never been greater, and it will be no less until we each take a part in the solution.

Lord,

help me to find the opportunities in my life
to speak out for those who cannot speak;
then guide me in my attempts to do this for You.
Amen.

Do not cast me off in the time of old age.

Psalm 71:9, NRSV

Senior Class

Robert S. Hampel

Today we are living longer. The number of senior citizens is growing rapidly. Many are residing in retirement facilities, where meals, housekeeping services, and a sense of security are provided. But some senior citizens continue to live alone in their own homes, by choice perhaps or because of the lack of funds or available space in affordable senior housing.

As in other churches and communities, some of us in a church in Newark, California, became concerned about older folks who seldom got out of their homes, who lacked the means of transportation they once had, and who had little contact with other people. We decided to ask some who fit this general description if they would like to have someone from the church call them on the phone each day to see if they were all right or if they needed anything. In responding, a number of these folks said that they thought this good idea was something needed, but they would like to be the ones doing the calling on others, not the ones being called.

Junior high young people in a nearby church are taking part in an "adopt-a-grandparent" outreach. But both these young people and the grandparents understand that this is not a one-way street. The older people welcome the young people and are encouraged to hear of the desire of these youth to serve the Lord. The young people are truly blessed by their adopted grandparents, some of whom have taught Sunday School for many years and all of whom have much to share of their walk with the Lord.

How easy it is to assume that those who are older can no longer contribute to a church or to a community as they may have done in the past. Until relatively recently, many seniors have been relegated to second-class citizenship. But as we have learned, that perspective can be changed.

Scripture is clear that God will not cast off people in their old age. We should do no less.

Heavenly Father,
to whom each person is special,
bless the witness of those who have walked with You
for many years.
Amen.

And let the peace of Christ rule in your hearts, to which indeed you were called in the one body.

Colossians 3:15, NRSV

A Memory of Peace

James H. Harrison

My dad worked for Pacific Telephone in Pasadena, California. I well remember his '53 Chevy troubleshooter truck, painted Bell Telephone green, with ladders on top and cupboards and drawers on the sides. On it I recall a bumper sticker depicting a ghostly figure saying, "Beware of SOND!" Dad said SOND was an acronym for September, October, November, and December. Bell Tel had determined these were the worst months for accidents because people were so busy. "Beware of SOND!" was a campaign to alert drivers to hazards.

My childhood eyes saw SOND as busy, but not hazardous. It was a time to return to school, to renew friendships and begin preparing for the holidays. During SOND our small Evangelical Lutheran Church hummed with activity. The people, programs, music, and worship experiences still bounce around in my memory. It was a time to focus on God as the Giver of all gifts and on the birth of our Lord and Savior.

Today people are busy all the time, not just during SOND, and busyness still creates hazards. Clergy and counselors agree busyness carries hazards for the family, as individual pursuits threaten the very structure of God's design for family unity. We know, because it threatened our family, too.

My wife and I were both consumed by our work, church, and community activities. Our teenagers were busy with school, church, and friends. We were moving in four separate directions. Disaster surely would have visited us, but one year during SOND I remembered Dad's truck and that bumper sticker. My mind wandered back to my childhood and my old church family and the joy we had because the peace of Christ ruled in our hearts.

As I stepped back into the present, my heart ached for my wife, my children, and Christ's peace. During dinner, I shared my memories and thoughts with them, adding, "I think we should beware of SOND!" The peace and joy of Christ had nearly been snatched from our family's hearts. We wanted it back!

We thanked God for slowing us down long enough to recognize the hazards we were facing. We prayed for the peace of Christ to come into our hearts. We declared, again, that we were a family in the body of Christ. And we all understood when after we finished eating and were sitting at the table talking, our daughter declared, "You know, guys, we don't need to beware of SOND. We just need to be aware of God!"

Dear God,
while everything around me goes so fast,
keep my spirit still so I can walk in quiet communion with You.
In Jesus' name.
Amen.

The Dividends of Fathering

R. Kent Hughes

I remember with technicolor clarity when our first child was born—August 10, 1963—a blazing hot southern California night. It had been so hot that day that I had taken my round little wife to the ocean to cool off. There I hollowed out a place in the sand for her tummy, and we stretched out under the sun while the cool breezes refreshed us—and unwittingly we both began to sunburn.

It was midafternoon when we headed back to the heat and smog of L.A., so we rolled back the sunroof of our VW and foolishly baked some more.

After dinner, as we lay smarting on the hot sheets of our bed, labor began, and that is about all we remember of our sunburns. My wife was occupied with another kind of pain, and I was so excited I forgot about mine. That night brought one of the greatest events of our lives—for God gave us our firstborn, a beautiful little girl we named Holly.

Another event has lodged in my mind with similar vividness. On July 23, 1986, twenty-three years later, in another hospital in far-off

Illinois, my baby Holly gave birth to her firstborn, a beautiful little boy, Brian, and his father held him with the same pride.

Both experiences were profoundly supernatural, for I saw God's creation.

Though just a speck on time's continuum, I felt a sacred solidarity with the past and the present. I also felt grace, the unhindered flow of God's goodness to me and my family.

I have mutually fulfilling relationships with all my children. They are independent of me, but they desire my company and counsel. We have mutual respect. They call me, and I call them, and we all live for the holidays when we can be together.

I have shared all this because, though I have not been a perfect father, I have learned some things along the way which I must pass along, man to man, to those of you in the midst or at the beginning of fathering.

Men, there are few places where sanctified sweat will show greater dividends than in fathering. If you are willing to work at it, you can be a good father. If you are willing to sweat, you will see abundant blessing.

Dear Lord,

teach me to be patient and diligent with my children

as You are with me.

Amen.

A Gift of Love

David P. Hauk

My son gave me my Father's Day gift today. It's a couple of days early, but that's all right.

He had wanted it to be a secret, but I knew what it was. I had been watching my boy through the window, and I had seen him pull the twig off the tree as he was walking along. He was in his own little world—his wonderful child world where everything is fascinating and cause for curiosity.

I stood and waited for him, watching him walk on the curb like a tightrope walker high above the net. His arms were stretched out at his sides for balance. He placed one foot slowly in front of the other. And his eyes were fixed on the path ahead.

Suddenly, he looked up and saw me watching. Quickly, he put his hand behind his back to conceal his treasure. He was off his tightrope now, running to me with a big smile on his face.

"Hi, Daddy!" he exclaimed. "This is for you. It's for Father's Day." Proudly, he brought his present out from behind his back.

I knelt down to give him a hug and kiss. "Thank you. That was really nice of you."

I was thrilled, not so much with the gift itself, but with the spirit in which it was given. I don't believe he had snatched the twig with the intention of giving it to me; he picked it just because it was a kid's thing to do. But without even thinking he unselfishly gave his newfound treasure to someone else to make them happy. It was a spontaneous act of love coming straight from the heart.

So, actually, this day my son gave me two Father's Day gifts. One was a leafy twig pulled off a tree—not very pretty and quick to die. The other was an example of true, unselfish love—a beautiful gift that will last forever.

Father,
help me to pass on the gift of Your love
freely and unselfishly.
Amen.

House and wealth are an inheritance from fathers,
but a prudent wife is from the Lord.

Proverbs 19:14, NASB

A Prudent Wife

Christopher Robert Johnson

It was probably the most chaotic time of my life: turning twenty-one, graduating from college, starting a career, buying a new car, and getting married, all within a six-month period. Youthful ambition and optimism made me want to experience all life had to offer in the shortest amount of time. I was ready to conquer the world, or so I thought.

I discovered, however, that a strange thing happens when the wedding is over, the last handful of rice is swept up, the tuxedo is returned to the rental shop, and the final thank-you card is addressed. The future is not as clear as it seemed. Now your decisions affect two lives. The nights out with the boys come to a screeching halt. The career path develops a fork. Whose job should take priority, his or hers?

The only way to breach post-honeymoon anxiety is to communicate with your new spouse. Fortunately, my wife is deeply caring, sympathetic, and understanding. She has always exercised great wisdom in our marriage. Without her shrewdness and consideration, the transformation from bachelor to husband would have been long and rocky.

Now that several years have passed since the day I vowed commitment to my wife, I realize the truth in the verse from Proverbs. Our society can provide a man with a "house and wealth," for the relative affluence of American society has made the accumulation of material goods possible. Those who are not fortunate enough to come from affluent families can still build wealth through their abilities and actions. However, no matter how rich and successful a man becomes, there is still nothing in his life that has the value of a prudent wife. An admirer, motivator, playmate, counselor, listener, decision maker, or shoulder to cry on—the prudent wife makes life's tempest bearable and life's jubilance memorable.

Truly, a prudent wife is an answered prayer and a blessing from God.

Lord,

help me to recognize those blessings You have bestowed upon me. Too often I see the house and riches
but fail to notice those gifts which mean the most.
Let me live a prudent life in all possible ways.

Amen.

As always Christ will be exalted in my body, whether by life or by death. For to me, to live is Christ and to die is gain.

Philippians 1:20–21, NIV

Final Words, Final Acts

Max Lucado

In a recent trip to my hometown I took some time to go see a tree. "A live oak tree," my dad called it (with the accent on "live"). It was nothing more than a sapling, so thin I could wrap my hand around it and touch my middle finger to my thumb.

"A special tree," I said to myself, "with a special job." I looked around. The cemetery was lined with elms but no oaks. The ground was dotted with tombstones but no trees. Just this one. A special tree for a special man.

About three years ago Daddy began noticing a steady weakening of his muscles. It began in his hands. He then felt it in his calves. Next his arms thinned a bit.

He mentioned his condition to my brother-in-law, who is a physician. My brother-in-law, alarmed, sent him to a specialist. The specialist conducted a lengthy battery of tests—blood, neurological, and muscular—and he reached his conclusion. Lou Gehrig's disease.

I looked down at the plot of ground that would someday entomb my father. Daddy always wanted to be buried under an oak tree so he bought this one.

The lump got tighter in my throat. A lesser man might have been angry. Another man might have given up. But Daddy didn't. He knew that his days were numbered so he began to get his house in order.

He improved the house for Mom by installing a sprinkler system and a garage door opener and by painting the trim. He got the will updated. He verified the insurance and retirement policies. He bought some stock to go toward his grandchildren's education. He planned his funeral. He bought cemetery plots for himself and Mom. He prepared his kids through words of assurance and letters of love. And last of all, he bought the tree. A live oak tree.

Final words. Final acts. Each one is a window through which the cross can be better understood. Each one opens a treasury of promises. "So that is where you learned it," I said aloud as though speaking to my father.

I looked one last time at the slender oak. I touched it as if it had been hearing my thought. "Grow," I whispered. "Grow strong. Stand tall. Yours is a valued treasure."

He was awake when I got home. I leaned over his bed. "I checked on the tree," I told him. "It's growing."

He smiled.

Lord,

give me the will and the way to live like my father.
He knew it was easier to die like Jesus,
because he lived like Him for a lifetime.
Thank You for allowing me to be his son.
Amen.

Listen children,

to a father's instruction, and be attentive,

that you may gain insight.

Proverbs 4:1, NRSV

The Benefit of Experience

Michael Martin

When the principal called a close friend of mine for a visit to the school office, my friend was in the midst of an important project. The interruption upset him. He was even more disturbed when he learned that his son had been caught with pornographic magazines in school. This was really a surprise; the boy was so young, innocent, and had never been in trouble before. He'd always attended Sunday School. He knew right from wrong. My friend found it hard to believe his son could do such a thing.

Then my friend remembered looking at such magazines when he was his son's age. It seemed that all the boys looked at these kinds of magazines and talked about sex. He recalled that often boys are pressured to say and do things they know to be wrong. His son was at the age where kids become curious about sex, just as he had been. Part of him said there was no reason to be angry with his son, "That's just the way boys are," he reasoned. But another part said that even though he, too, may have done it as a kid, it still wasn't right. Clearly, the situation had to be handled very carefully.

At home my friend told his son he understood what he was going through. He also told him he had the responsibility to give him the benefit of what he'd learned as an adult.

My friend admitted that many of the things he'd done as a boy were wrong, too. My friend told his son, "I'll try to help you avoid those mistakes."

Becoming a man involves more than just getting older. In the process you examine and discard many naive and foolish ideas from childhood. Although it's important to understand why boys do what they do, fathers must give them the benefit of what they have learned. We must guide our sons as they try to determine right from wrong.

Lord,
give me the wisdom to profit from and make use of the lessons
You have taught me.
Amen.

A new commandment I give to you, that you love one another, even as I have loved you.

John 13:34, NASB

A Special Kind of Love

Josh McDowell

I had a lot of hatred in my life. It wasn't something outwardly manifested, but there was a kind of inward grinding. I was ticked off with people, with things, with issues. Like so many other people, I was insecure. Every time I met someone different from me, he became a threat to me.

But I hated one man more than anyone else in the world—my father. I hated his guts. To me he was the town alcoholic. If you're from a small town and one of your parents is an alcoholic, you know what I'm talking about. Everybody knows. My friends would come to high school and make jokes about my father being downtown. They didn't think it bothered me. I was like other people, laughing on the outside, but let me tell you, I was crying on the inside. I'd go out in the barn and see my mother beaten so badly she couldn't get up, lying in the manure behind the cows. When we had friends over, I would take my father out, tie him up in the barn, and park the car up around the silo. We would tell our friends he'd had to go somewhere. I don't think anyone could have hated any more than I hated my father.

After I made my decision for Christ, a love from God through Jesus Christ entered my life and was so strong it took that hatred and turned it upside down. I was able to look my father squarely in the eyes and say, "Dad, I love you." And I really meant it. After some of the things I'd done, that shook him up.

When I transferred to a private university I was in a serious car accident. My neck in traction, I was taken home. I'll never forget my father coming into my room. He asked me, "Son, how can you love a father like me?" I said, "Dad, six months ago I despised you." Then I shared with him my conclusions about Jesus Christ: "Dad, I let Christ come into my life. I can't explain it completely but as a result of that relationship I've found the capacity to love and accept not only you but other people just the way they are."

Forty-five minutes later one of the greatest thrills of my life occurred. Somebody in my own family, someone who knew me so well I couldn't pull the wool over his eyes, said to me, "Son, if God can do in my life what I've seen him do in yours, then I want to give Him the opportunity." Right there my father prayed with me and trusted Christ.

Dear Lord,
thank You for coming into my life
and allowing me to love others with Your kind of love.
Amen.

Freshly Brewed

Louis Merryman

There have been times when I have wondered if my sons were truly a reward from God or a just and well-deserved punishment. There were days when they were in total rebellion and days when I went out of my way to provoke them. Then, too, there were the overnight fishing trips and visits to the Magic Kingdom.

My oldest son liked to do things his way. When he was high-chair age he would hand me his plate and glass after he was finished eating and drinking. The problem was the hand-off from the high chair to my hand, which lasted only about a second. He'd let go and the plate would crash to the floor. Some of his actions got worse in high school, and my response wasn't always the right one. There were days when we wondered if we'd make it to his manhood. We did.

My sons are grown now. Two of them joined me for a recent winter vacation in ski country. It was a real vacation with no schedules. We stayed up late and slept in. Our first morning there I fully understood the meaning of children being God's reward when I woke up to the aroma of a freshly brewed pot of coffee and enough bacon and eggs to feed a small army.

I believe that love is demonstrated in small, specific acts. For me, in this earthly realm, there is no greater demonstration of love than to be the first one awake and to brew coffee for everyone else. There is also no greater joy in beginning a day than to wake up to the aroma of freshly brewed coffee, prepared by a loved one.

If there's spilled milk in your home today—at the hand of one of your children—remember that today's milk drinker is tomorrow's coffee brewer. There is hope.

Father God,

thank You for my children.

Forgive me for my trespasses against them.

Thank You for Your words which teach me to teach them.

Stand next to me as I grow them up.

In Jesus' name.

Amen.

I pray that you, being rooted and established in love,
may have power…to grasp how wide and long and high and deep is
the love of Christ.

Ephesians 3:17–18, NIV

Enormous Love

Dennis V. Meyers

I know a man who married, at the age of twenty-four, a young lady of twenty-two. This young lady had a fifteen-month-old daughter whose father had been killed in an automobile accident prior to her birth. That little girl had never had a daddy. Now that she finally did, she was really excited.

The child loved her new daddy and emulated his every action. She would ask for "a salad like Daddy's." She would wipe her mouth with her napkin "like Daddy" did.

There was only one problem. This new daddy didn't treat his little angelic, full-of-life bundle of joy as a father should. He didn't recognize or appreciate the gift he'd been given.

In disciplining her, he'd sometimes spank a little harder than necessary. Using her flinching in fear and cowering as an excuse, he'd spank her more. He always seemed to require more from her than could be expected for her age. And she? She put all of her little heart into trying to please her daddy.

As she grew into a young lady and the need for spankings passed, her daddy still expected her to be error-free. And she? She still gave it everything she had, continuing to seek his approval.

That little girl has grown up to be a fine young woman. She's married and is expecting her own child.

What amazes this daddy is, through the years, she always loved him, and still does.

The example set by this young woman has given me insight into how wide and long and high and deep the Lord's love is for us! We, like the daddy, who are so undeserving, are loved so much.

Lord,

thank You for Your enormous love.

Help me to love others unconditionally.

Amen.

Therefore, since we are surrounded by such a great cloud of winesses,
let us throw off everything that hinders
and the sin that so easily entangles,
and let us run with perseverance the race marked out for us.

Hebrews 12:1, NIV

Does Anyone Really Care?

Patrick M. Morley

One evening we threw a going away party for Ragne (RAWG-nee). For one whole year Ragne had soaked up American culture like a sponge.

A pastor from Sweden, he had journeyed to America to learn how to make his own country come alive for God. Several of us attended a weekly Bible study in our home. Part of Ragne's training was to participate with us. His insights, always peppered with humor, livened up our group.

On our last evening together, we went around the room and each person said their farewells to Ragne, and then we presented him an engraved pen-and-pencil set for his desk back home in Sweden.

When all were finished, I asked Ragne to tell us the most interesting thing he had learned about Americans.

Without hesitation he said in a thick, Scandinavian accent, "Well, when I first got here, everywhere I would go, everyone would always say to me, 'Ragne, so good to see you. How are you doing?'

"It took me about six months to realize—nobody wants an answer!"

Sad, but true. We have all experienced the sting of the insincere inquiry. Why doesn't anyone want an answer? For some, of course, it's just a social greeting, but for most of us we can see a clue into how we live.

We Americans are so busy, so over-committed, so up to our ears in duties and debts—we just don't want to know. We have so many problems of our own that there is no time left for anyone else. We just don't have the time to "want an answer."

More than a few men are swamped, in over their heads. After taking care of their own problems they have no capacity left over to help anyone else. They don't understand why they are so caught up in the rat race, and their lives are frequently spinning out of control.

It was fifty years ago, in 1939, when Christopher Morley penned the words in his novel *Kitty Foyle*, "Their own private life gets to be like a rat race." Many of us today are trying to win the wrong race.

We could view Ragne's perceptive remark as an indictment, but instead, let's use it as a springboard to look into the problems, issues, and temptations that face the man in the mirror every day and see what practical solutions we can discover for winning the right race.

Dear God,
make me more appreciative of my brothers and sisters.
Give me the sensitivity to let them know
I really do care how they are doing,
just as I might want them to know how I'm doing, too.
Amen.

Love is patient, love is kind…It is not rude.

1 Corinthians 13:4–5, NIV

Impatience

Al Munger

She was driving an old station wagon and had pulled into the only lane that would accommodate our fifth wheel trailer at my favorite gas station. I decided to wait in the street, with lights flashing, to alert the cars in the lane behind me.

She got out, found the gas cap locked, fetched her keys from the ignition and removed the cap, all in slow motion. Looking in the mirror I could see a string of cars coming up behind me. My recreational vehicle was blocking the curb lane.

After squeezing the nozzle with no results she read the sign, "Prepay before pumping." Getting her purse, she lined up at the pay booth. Sauntering back to her car, she filled the tank and hung up the hose.

"Let's see," I said to myself, "seven cars waiting. Boy, I sure wish she would hurry."

After getting her change, the lady got into the car but couldn't find her keys. I could see them dangling from the gas cap. I waited. I fumed. I fretted about blocking the street.

I wondered what those drivers were saying about "RV people."

Finally, she discovered her keys and started the motor, but then she had a difficult time shifting into low gear. By now, fifteen minutes had passed. At last, she pulled away from the pump, but the street was now filled with cars waiting for the light to change. I was steaming.

We faced off through our windshields at ten paces. "Come on. Get going!" I said as I waved her out of the way.

She looked at me with hurt in her eyes. Trying to move quickly, she stalled the engine. Finally, she pulled away, avoiding my eyes and my sour face.

Then God whispered to me, "Love is patient, love is kind, love is not rude," and I knew in an instant that I'd just reinforced her stereotype of the insensitive, arrogant male.

Pulling up to the gas pump I looked up the street. The back of her station wagon was fading in the distance. Suddenly I wanted to go after her, talk to her, and say, "I'm so sorry. I knew you were having a hard time. Please forgive me for being so impatient, so rude." But she was gone.

Lord,

forgive me for being such an inferior example of Your love.

Please comfort those who we treat improperly

And, Jesus, help me to think less of myself and more of others—

especially those who can't find their keys to the ignition.

Amen.

Be imitators of God, therefore,
as dearly loved children and live a life of love,
just as Christ loved us and gave himself up for us
as a fragrant offering and sacrifice to God.

Ephesians 5:1–2, NIV

Role Models

Gerry Presley

When reflecting on our times and the troubles we face as a nation and a society, I began to think about how we become what we are as individuals. I thought about how important role models are to all of us, but I realized they're much more important to our children.

Our kids today don't really know what role models are. They look at television personalities and athletes and rock singers and all different types of people and take into their minds a lot of ideas about the way people act.

I wonder if our children ever look to us, their parents, as role models. Do they? This question is important. It's important to our children.

Have you ever sat down with your child and said, "In the midst of all our living together, and in the midst of all that I don't do perfectly, you can look to me to be your role model"? Have you deliberately taken the time to do that? Have you ever said, "You can look to me. I'll be the model for you. I'll make mistakes, but in God's grace, you can look to me to be your example"?

"Someday, when you want to know how to love your wife, look and see how I love your mother.

"When you want to know how to love your neighbor across the street or how to love your friends, look to me and I'll be the model for how to do that." That's gets scary, doesn't it!

I realized that I'd never done that with my children. I never sat down and had that kind of specific conversation. Oh, we had lots of conversations, but I never said to them, "You can look to me to be your role model. I'll disappoint you at times. I'll make mistakes, but I will not fail you. In God's grace, and with His support, I will not fail you."

As Christians, we want to change our world. We want to be in a world that's different tomorrow and the next day, a world that's better for our children and for us. It'll take deliberate action on our part. It really will. God wants us to be the kind of models for our children they can look to and trust in confidence. We must be committed as the body of believers to being models as husbands, as parents, as friends, and as neighbors.

Father,
my heart's desire is to exemplify unto all who cross my path daily
the quality of love that You and Jesus share together.
Develop me into a model of Your likeness
that I may change the world I live in and glorify You.
In Jesus' name.
Amen.

There are varieties of gifts, but the same Spirit. And there are varieties of ministries, and the same Lord. And there are varieties of effects, but the same God who works all things in all persons.

1 Corinthians 12:4–6, NASB

The Difference in Being Different

Jason Presley

Since the first day of school, I knew Jonathan was different. I spotted him walking around, holding a tattered black Bible, grinning shamelessly and singing worship songs at a volume and sincerity that made me a little uncomfortable. He even looked different. His secondhand clothes and disheveled appearance contrasted the school's wealthy, stylish majority.

Later that year, the music department held a choral concert celebrating Black gospel songs and hymns. About five minutes into the show, one individual suddenly stood out. It was Jonathan, and he was singing with all his might—his eyes closed, his neck outstretched, his body swaying unconsciously, and his entire face beaming with undeniable joy. I noticed others around me were watching him as well. Some laughed mockingly, some smiled condescendingly, some even frowned, but inside me, something clicked, and I found myself admiring this uninhibited peer with such a passion for music and for God. When the concert ended, I hunted him down, shook his hand, and told him how much I enjoyed watching him sing. He grinned, and a small connection formed.

The year ended and I was off for summer study in Russia. At the airport, I was pleasantly surprised when Jonathan showed up, for he too was going to Russia. Over the next five weeks, a friendship developed as we spent our evenings exchanging music and songs.

However, these discussions were the only times I ever saw Jonathan. After the first week, it became apparent his agenda for this trip differed greatly from the rest of ours. While we visited mind-boggling museums, Jonathan visited a struggling evangelical church. While we absorbed renowned Russian ballets, he absorbed the hearts and humble homes of people in the small congregation. When we traveled to ancient monasteries and fortresses, he traveled all over the city with individuals in the church. By our third week, he was teaching a midweek Bible study and preaching on Sunday. Many in our group misunderstood Jonathan's alienation, but when I asked him why he never joined us, he smiled and said that the Russian people took precedent over the culture and that he wanted to serve rather than observe.

My first impression of Jonathan remains true to this day. He is different. But through him I have learned not only to appreciate uniqueness, but also to understand that often in order to make a difference, God calls us to be different.

Lord,

I praise You for my unique personality.

Help me to rejoice in the diversity of mankind,

and give me courage, like Your Son, Jesus,

to risk being misunderstood or ridiculed by others

for being different in order to follow Your agenda for my life.

Amen.

Be merciful to me,
O Lord, for I am in distress;
my eyes grow weak with sorrow,
my soul and my body with grief.

Psalm 31:9, NIV

Breaking the Silent Grief

Brad Sargent

I never knew my father's best friend. I heard Dad mention his name perhaps twenty times in thirty years, always giving his first name and middle initial. On those rare occasions when I talked with Dad about Patrick J., he'd only say a few sentences at the most. I can recall only the sketchiest of details from his comments.

Patrick J. and Dad had been buddies in the early forties. They were stationed together during World War II. They joked a lot and drank a lot together. Patrick J. was killed in the war. Other bits of information I may have heard only once I can't remember. However, what I remember distinctly was the absence of any reflection of sorrow or grief in my Dad's recollections. It seems to me to be peculiar to his generation.

Why wasn't Dad's generation more public with their grief? Certainly his generation of men had much sorrow. They lived through the Great Depression and half a decade in a world war. What unspoken rules forced them to gag their mourning? Did they consider it unmanly? How might life have been different for us, their sons, if they'd put more words to their feelings, as did the psalmist David?

I'm facing my own shower of grief these days, sadly, without much training or example. Dad's gone now. I'm also in the process of packing to move a long way from home, leaving my mother, my church family, and good friends from a Christian men's support group.

Perhaps hardest of all will be the separation in miles from my best friend of seventeen years, Bob, and his family. No more freewheeling, face-to-face discussions about music, theology, life, or men's issues in America and the church.

Maybe I'm understanding Dad's silent grief over Patrick J. Carmody a little better these days. But I also hope to be more like David by breaking the silence and turning to the Lord.

Father God,
help me embrace sadness as part of life
that increases my hunger for You
and for eventually being reunited with loved ones in heaven.
Help me to work through my grief,
not being afraid to show others my sorrows.
Amen.

And this is the boldness we have in him,

that if we ask anything according to his will, he hears us.

And if we know that he hears us in whatever we ask,

we know that we have obtained the requests made of him.

1 John 5:14–15, NRSV

My Name Is Not Daddy-Daddy

Scott Sibley

"Daddy-Daddy, can you please get me a drink?" There was no impatience in my four-year-old son's voice. But when he called to me, he didn't even hesitate or pause for a second. He said it as though it were my whole name.

"My name's not Daddy-Daddy," I corrected him. I knew then I needed to be corrected, too. He'd changed my name to "Daddy-Daddy" because he found that one "Daddy" wasn't enough to get my attention. I was too busy or too preoccupied or I just wasn't very interested in what he wanted to say.

Since God is the original example of a father, the relationship we have with our earthly father can determine how we relate to Him. The good things we see in our father can help us to love God. The father's shortcomings must be overcome as we try to understand and get to know God better.

I don't often think of God as my Father. Many times I don't have the confidence that He hears me. And I'm not sure I understand what it means that we "obtain the requests made of Him." But it sounds like a great promise, and I'd like to learn more and more about it.

I do know that I love my son and it hurts to realize I haven't been listening to him. So when I asked him not to call me "Daddy-Daddy," I also resolved to listen more carefully and respond more quickly. And I hope it helps him understand that God hears and answers when we call on Him.

Father,

thank You for the promise that You hear me and answer.

Build in me the confidence of Your love.

Let me believe Your promise that I will obtain my requests from You.

Amen.

Humble yourselves, therefore, under God's mighty hand,
that he may lift you up in due time.
Cast all your anxiety on him because he cares for you.

1 Peter 5:6–7, NIV

Cry for Help

Michael Slater

I remember an incident that took place a few years ago at Huntington Beach. The summer day was beautiful, the sun was warm, and it felt good to be down by the ocean.

I walked into the water to do a little bodysurfing.

After riding a few waves, I began the long swim back toward shore. Suddenly, I noticed something unusual about another swimmer. He was a young man, about thirteen years of age, and maybe twenty-five yards in front of me. He was struggling against the waves, and as I watched him I knew something was very wrong! I quickly swam over to him, grabbed him, and towed him back to the beach where we were both out of danger.

Bringing him to safety had proved to be no easy task, and afterward we both sat on the sand for awhile, exhausted. In a few moments I introduced myself, and he told me his name was Steve.

When we finally caught our breath I asked him a question. "Steve, were you drowning out there?"

He bent his head and looked down at the sand. He hesitated and then answered, "Yes." Even though we had come through this experience together, this young man felt so embarrassed that he could not even look at me one-on-one. He could not look me in the eye!

After a moment I asked him a second question. "Steve, since you felt you were drowning, why didn't you cry out for help?"

Almost immediately he turned, looked at me and said, "Cry out for help, Mike? What would my friends think if I cried out for help?"

I sat there stunned. I could not believe what I had heard! How foolish, I thought. In another minute Steve would have drowned. Yet, no matter what, he would not have cried out for help! He was going to make it on his own or not make it at all.

Why is it that, like that young man at Huntington Beach, so many people find it difficult to say, "Help, I need you! I need encouragement. I need support. I don't think I can do it alone"? Why do people refuse to reach out for help and support? Why do we find it hard to admit we need encouragement?

Father,
I need You. I need Your help.
I know I cannot go through life alone.
I'm so glad You've provided brothers in the Lord
who will stand by me, support me,
and reach out to me even when I'm unable to ask.
Amen.

*But the fruit of the Spirit
is love, joy, peace, patience, kindness, goodness, faithfulness,
gentleness, self-control.*

Galatians 5:22–23, NASB

Please, Be Tender

Gary Smalley

I normally become completely oblivious to my family and the world when I'm near a stream, totally "submerging" myself in the exhilarating environment of fishing.

[Once] when we pulled up in our minimotor home beside a beautiful stream, my heart was pounding. I could hardly wait to get my reel rigged up. First, I rigged the kids' reels and told them, "Look, if you get tangled up, you're on your own."

I found the perfect spot: a nice deep hole in a pool in front of a big boulder. I threw in the lure and let it wander naturally to the bottom of the pool. It swirled around and WHAM! I got my first trout. I had nearly caught the limit when Greg came running up. I was sure he was about to jump into the stream and spook the fish. "Dad," he yelled anxiously, "Kari broke her leg!"

Kari broke her leg? What a time to break her leg! I couldn't believe she would do this to me. It was hard for me to leave, but I gave the line to Greg and said, "Don't break it. Don't get it tangled up. Just keep it in there." I ran in Kari's direction, avoiding the big pool. After all, I didn't want to scare the fish.

Downstream, Kari was crying, "Daddy, I think I broke my leg."

"Don't touch it," I said. "It's not broken; it's just bruised. Put your leg in this cold water to soak for a few minutes."

I'm really embarrassed to tell the rest of the story, but maybe you can learn from my insensitivity. I ran back to the fishing hole and caught a few more trout before walking back to where Kari was crying. "Dad, this water is cold."

I rather roughly got her up to walk, but she couldn't. When I tried to hoist her up on the bank and couldn't, she started crying again and said, "Dad, you're so rough with me. Can't you be tender?" Something flashed when she said that word. It reminded me of all the times my wife and other women have told me, "What we need is tenderness and gentleness, not harshness. We don't need lectures." And I couldn't even be tender with my eleven-year-old daughter. I had already lectured Kari because I felt she was interrupting my day. "Why didn't you look first?" I had asked her.

When I came to my senses, I hung my head low and said, "Kari, I've been so wrong to be harsh with you. I really feel bad. Would you forgive me?"

We just held each other for a while, and then she looked up into my eyes and asked gently, "Dad, did you use deodorant today?"

Lord,

even when I know better, I must be reminded

that it is Your gentle love that we all need so very much.

As a father and a husband, a brother and a friend,

remind me to be as sensitive to others

as I know You will always be with me.

Amen.

An excellent wife, who can find?
For her worth is far above jewels.
The heart of her husband trusts in her.

Proverbs 31:10–11, NASB

Behind Every Successful Man

Lester W. Smith

After considerable prayer I entered graduate school as a part-time student. At the time I was employed with the federal government as a personnel management specialist, but I sensed the calling of our Lord into some form of full-time Christian vocation.

Although I considered myself to be a Christian who was well-versed in the Scriptures, I'd never spent a day in Bible college. My undergraduate degree was earned at a secular university. As a result, I quickly learned that I was considerably overmatched by my classmates. All of my fellow students were already pastors or graduates of a Bible college or both. I felt totally overwhelmed. Theological terms were tossed casually about during each class session by both students and teachers, terms that I'd never heard of as a layman.

After two weeks of stress and frustration over being a fish out of water, I came home from class and announced to my wife I was going to drop out of school.

"No, you won't," she said simply and matter-of-factly.

"It's no use," I tried to persuade her. "I don't understand prelapsarian, hypostatic union, exegesis, and all that other stuff."

But she persisted. She reminded me that we had prayed about the matter of my going back to school, and she insisted that, with the help of God, I would succeed.

And since we'd fully paid the tuition for my classes, I resigned myself to completing the semester. But there was no question in my mind, I would *not* be returning for any additional courses.

Much to my surprise, my wife was right. As the semester progressed, I managed to grasp the terminology. In fact, I outscored all of my classmates on the final exam and went on to complete the program and graduate.

Since then, I've wondered how things would have worked out if we as men had listened more often to godly counsel from our wives. God may be using them to speak to us. When we neglect to give serious consideration to the counsel and concerns of our mates, we may be missing out on guidance and direction from the Holy Spirit.

Gracious Lord,
help me to remember
that You just may be speaking through my spouse
when she offers her advice.
Amen.

Behold, how good and how pleasant it is
for brothers to dwell together in unity!

Psalm 133:1, NASB

Can't We All Just Get Along?

Robert C. Smith

Several days after the April 29, 1992, Los Angeles riot, people came together from all walks of life and from all races in an attempt to help clean up the debris and aid the victims of the riot in putting their lives back together.

As a pastor in the Los Angeles area, what really impressed me the most was how Christians came together. Suburban and urban churches united. We were able to put our cross-cultural differences aside and work together to help heal the hurts of the people. White pastors in suburbia called Black pastors in the inner city and offered their support. Many of these churches ended up working together throughout the week and then worshiping together on Sunday. We were having a great time fellowshiping with our white, brown, and yellow Christian brethren. In fact, we were having such a good time that I was tempted to ask God to send another riot if that's what it takes to get the church to function as it should. However, as the embers slowly turned cold, so did most of the fellowshiping. What happened?

The Lord reminded me that it may take a riot to get us together, but only godly love and caring will build lasting relationships. Therefore, I've decided to make myself a committee of one and attempt to establish genuine relationships with Christians in other races. Senator Bill Bradley of New Jersey said on one occasion, "If you don't have a friend of another race then you are part of the race problem."

I'm convinced that Jesus wants all Christians to get along. And I've found that the best way to love individuals of another race—as the Lord Jesus commands us to do—is to make friends with some of its people. I have a white friend and together we have made a commitment to meet once a month for prayer and fellowship. I am persuaded that if there is going to be unity in the Body, the churches of all races must learn to work together. Can't we all just get along?

Lord,

help me, as part of the church,

to put my cultural differences aside

and work together with others as one Body

in order to help reconcile men to You.

Amen.

For I consider that the sufferings of this present time
are not worthy to be compared with the glory
that is to be revealed to us.

Romans 8:18, NASB

Togetherness Brings Joy

Russell E. Spray

We had traveled for two days and were nearing our destination. Soon, after many months we would be reunited with my parents. The trip had been long and tiresome, for we had traveled through mid-summer heat without benefit of air-conditioning. The great wheat belt stretched behind us for many miles as we drove across this massive midwestern section of the country.

When night fell, we could easily see the sky because of the scarcity of trees. It seemed the stars shone more brightly than usual. We gazed through the darkness, which had settled down on the vast plains, and caught sight of twinkling lights in the distance.

It was the small Kansas town where my parents lived. What a welcomed beacon! We forgot the difficulties of the journey. Our weariness vanished. Knowing we were nearing our destination, we could scarcely contain our joy.

Together we broke into song. As we traveled those last few miles, my wife, two daughters, and I sang lustily. "Home, Sweet Home," we crooned at the top of our voices. Yes, at last we could see the lights of the city shining ever so brightly.

Christians often grow weary on their journey through this life. The pilgrimage becomes long and treacherous as we travel over mountains of trial and temptation and down into valleys of sorrow and disappointment. We become footsore and tired. But the trials of this life will be forgotten when we near the end of this life's journey.

The way, rugged though it may be, is made lighter, however, if we have developed family togetherness. Having loved ones to depend upon for support eases the pain of the journey. Knowing they are ready to accompany us to the very end and beyond adds joy and comfort and strengthens our well-being.

As we near the end of our journey, we'll see the lights of the city of God shining in the distance. What a thrill that will be to join together and sing the song of the redeemed. All the sufferings of this present world will be forgotten as we wing our way into our heavenly home.

Dear Father in heaven,
thank You for bringing my family
through many difficulties and circumstances.
Thank You for the assurance given us by the apostle Paul.
The trials, troubles, and testings of this life will not compare
with the glory that shall be revealed to us.
Amen.

As long as Moses held up his hands,
the Israelites were winning,
but whenever he lowered his hands,
the Amalekites were winning.

Exodus 17:11, NIV

Give that Man a Hand

John Strubhar

Let me set the scene for you.

Moses and the people of God were involved in a battle against the Amalekites, a fierce group of fighting people who roamed the northern Sinai deserts. As long as Moses held up his hands, God's people under Joshua were in command. However, as the battle raged on, Moses became weary. His hands were so heavy he could no longer hold them up. So great was his fatigue that he could not continue standing. He had to sit on a large stone.

As his arms tired and his hands drooped to his sides, the momentum swung to Amalek and his insidious hosts. It looked as if Israel would be defeated! But into the thick of the battle and in the face of personal fatigue and exhaustion came two trusted friends, Aaron and Hur, who did for Moses what he couldn't do for himself. They held up his hands and provided support, one on either side of him. As they held up Moses' hands, Joshua and the armies of Israel prevailed and the Amalekites were soundly turned back.

This historic account of God's miraculous intervention on behalf of the nation of Israel leaves a significant impression on my mind, especially when I consider the traditional way men approach life: alone!

The lone ranger approach doesn't work! Toughing it out by myself is a sure ticket to spiritual defeat. Relying on my human willpower and energy is insufficient when the stakes in life are stacked against me. Believe me, like every other guy, I've done it. The battle scars I've received are many. Moses couldn't conquer the situation he was facing alone, and neither can I. In a word, friendship is indispensable!

I'm more convinced than ever that as we race toward the twenty-first century, burnout and stress will not be far behind. What I need during these times is other men who will come alongside me, encourage me, pray for me, and join me in the battles I face.

It is the combined strength of God and His strength through trusted friends that enables me not only to survive, but to triumph when adversity and difficulty come my way.

The helping hands of friends made the difference for Moses. This same kind of personal involvement with others is making a difference for me.

Lord,
I confess that relationships with others don't come easily for me.
I tend to go it alone only to feel discouraged and depleted in spirit.
Help me to risk involvement in the lives of those
You bring into my life.
May I not only be a friend to someone today,
but also lift the hands of my fellow strugglers.
Amen.

Truly, truly, I say to you,
the Son can do nothing of Himself,
unless it is something He sees the Father doing.

John 5:19, NASB

My Dad

Charles R. Swindoll

My dad died last night.

He left as he had lived—quietly, graciously, and with dignity. Without demands or harsh words or even a frown, he surrendered himself—a tired, frail, humble gentleman—into the waiting arms of his Savior. Death, selfish and cursed enemy of man, won another battle.

As I stroked the hair from his forehead and kissed him good-bye, a hundred boyhood memories played around in my head: when I learned to ride a bike, he was there; when I wrestled with the multiplication table, his quick wit erased the hassle; when I discovered the adventure of driving a car, he was near, encouraging me; when I got my first job (delivering newspapers), he informed me how to increase my subscriptions and win the prize; when I mentioned a young woman I had fallen in love with, he pulled me aside and talked straight about being responsible for her welfare and happiness; when I did a hitch in the Marine Corps, the discipline I had learned from him made the transition easier.

Last night I realized I had him to thank for my deep love for America. And for knowing how to tenderly care for my wife. And for laughing at impossibilities. And for some of the habits I have picked up, like approaching people with a positive spirit rather than a negative one, staying with a task until it is finished, taking good care of my personal belongings, keeping my shoes shined, speaking up rather than mumbling, respecting authority, and standing alone (if necessary) in support of my personal convictions rather than giving in to more popular opinions. For these things I am deeply indebted to the man who raised me.

Admittedly, much of my dad's instruction was indirect—by model rather than by explicit statement. I do not recall his overt declarations of love as clearly as I do his demonstrations of it. His life revolved around my mother, the darling and delight of his life. Of that I am sure. When she left over nine years ago, something of him died as well. And so—to her he has been joined and they are, together, with our Lord, in the closest possible companionship one can imagine.

Lord,

I am forever grateful for all that my father on earth gave to me and forever grateful for all that You have given me.

I pray I'll always share as readily as both of you have done with me.

Amen.

Let all bitterness and wrath and anger and clamor and slander,
be put away from you, along with all malice.
And be kind to one another, tender-hearted, forgiving each other,
just as God in Christ also has forgiven you.

Ephesians 4:31–32, NASB

A Path to Peace

Fred W. Van Nice

The words above can be hard to live by. But, difficult as it may appear to be, I have found them to bring peace and healing in my life following a difficult relationship.

Having walked down the path of divorce and ugly child custody disputes, I can honestly say that I have felt toward my ex-wife all of the emotions the apostle Paul talks about.

As many divorcees know, broken marriages can become adversarial battlegrounds. Often, one parent is made to look like the bad guy. I too felt placed in this position.

I love my children very much. The sense of loss I have felt has been overwhelming at times and has caused my personal and professional life to suffer greatly. Anger, bitterness, wrath, and the temptation to speak evil against the mother of my children are all feelings I have experienced.

As Paul writes to the Ephesians about unity in the church, he counsels them about feelings that get in the way that not only can destroy the church, but also prevent them from having unity with God. As Moses taught the Israelites and Jesus taught the multitudes, we are to love God with all of our hearts. That's the first and greatest commandment. But it's impossible to do when negative feelings reside in our hearts.

Stop and think. Who are we hurting the most by carrying around feelings of bitterness, anger, and malice? We're the ones who suffer most with inner turmoil and bitterness, and we're unable to love God with our whole hearts.

Paul offers counsel on how to respond to one another. He says, "Be kind to one another, tenderhearted, forgiving one another, even as God for Christ's sake hath forgiven you."

Forgiveness means releasing the other person from his or her debt. At the same time, it releases you from anger and bitterness. Can you see the power in forgiveness? We have the power to release ourselves from those ugly feelings! And in so doing, we allow ourselves to move forward in other relationships, including our relationship with God.

In forgiveness I found peace. In peace I found my ability to love again. What a wonderful gift forgiveness is—not only to those toward whom you feel anger and bitterness, but more beneficially, to yourself.

Heavenly Father,
I praise and thank You for showing me how to forgive.
I lift up to You each and every person who suffers
from a broken relationship, especially the children.
I ask that You show each of them what You have shown me,
and help them find the freedom to love through forgiveness.
Amen.

Not that I have already obtained all this,
or have already been made perfect,
but I press on to take hold of that
for which Christ Jesus took hold of me.

Philippians 3:12, NIV

Tender Warrior

Stu Weber

If you're going to be a man after God's heart, you're not going to pretend to be perfect. Nobody is. So my kids need to know that I have needs, too. They need to understand that I'm not everything I want to be. I need to share with them not only my strengths and my "strong, silent character." I need to share with them, as they grow, my weaknesses and struggles, even failures—when it's appropriate. People around us need to know we're not Clark Kent, that life is not an exact science. We don't have it all together and it's important that we become healthily transparent with one another.

Genuine openness is a form of spirit-to-spirit communication that defies description—let alone definition. But you know it when you see it. I recall a moment in the life of my middle son.

Blake was just a youngster. I was mowing our yard astride our new lawn tractor. To an eight-year-old boy, such a contraption represents nirvana—to sit on it, to steer it, to *drive* it. Well, what else is there on this earth that matters? But in this case it wasn't happening because this safety-conscious "mean ol' dad" wouldn't allow him to ride it for fear of an accident and injury.

So Blake sat on the front porch and watched me on my rounds. Elbows on knees, head in hands, disappointment and longing written all over his little face—his gaze followed me back and forth across the yard, as if he was watching a tennis match (a very slow one). His posture cried out, *Oh, Daddy, I want to be WITH you!*

Ultimately, I could stand it no longer. This father's heart caved in. With a smile and an upraised arm, I motioned him to join me. His face burst into expression. He leaped off the porch, covering what seemed to be ten yards in a single bound. He flew to my side. Carefully, he climbed onto the seat safely between my knees. As he did, he slid forward and dropped his head back to look up at my face. I bent forward to look in his, our noses about six inches apart. His eyes literally sparkled. His soul came right to the surface. I saw deep down inside those eyes to his spirit, and he to mine.

Without a word, we communicated. Deeply. *I'm with you, and you're with me. We're doing the wonderful things together. I would rather be right here right now than any other place in the universe.*

It was a moment of open spiritual communication I will never forget.

Dear God,
my children are a sacred gift from You,
and an opportunity unlike any other You provide.
Remind me of my treasures here on earth
and for my responsibility to care for each of them
as You care for me.
Amen.

For the Father loves the Son and shows him all that he does. Yes, to your amazement he will show him even greater things than these.

John 5:20, NIV

Uncharted Territory

Levern Wedeven

Our house's leaky roof needed its blistered, curling shingles replaced. *It'll be expensive,* I thought, *unless we make it a family project.*

I expected great things from my fourteen-year-old son, Graham, who was past due for some construction experience and real physical labor.

"Watch," I said as we stood on the roof. "This is how a pitch fork and shovel peel off old shingles."

As soon as I finished the demonstration, I heard splashes in the swimming pool. His response to the call to work was one of flight. My example obviously wasn't a sufficient incentive.

The next day, however, we had helpers. That more social atmosphere kept Graham on the job. He learned each step involved in the roofing process.

"How about helping me roll felt onto the exposed deck?" I asked.

"Sure, Dad," was his reply.

Graham worked hard and periodically checked our progress. His capacity for work seemed to have expanded. He could now balance a full bundle of shingles on his shoulder as he ascended the ladder without hesitation.

He hardly noticed his blistering hands and pouring sweat because of the joy of working with others. I sensed his feeling of satisfaction. Work seemed to have taken on new meaning.

Before the project was completed, my vacation days ended.

"Graham," I said, "could you work alone while I'm not here?"

"Sure," he said.

When I returned from work the next day, I found he'd made astonishing progress. To my surprise, his techniques for chalking lines, laying shingles, and trimming edges were better than my own.

"Graham," I said, "I'm proud of you." The grin on his face told me that he was blessed by answering the call to work.

As I think about this father-and-son experience, it reminds me how my Lord and Father is trying to call me to His work. My answer is most often one of flight. But my Christian friends keep me accountable.

If I'm obedient, my son will do the same to accomplish much for the Lord's kingdom. My son could even surpass me. And our Father in heaven will then lead both of us into uncharted territory.

Lord,

give me the courage to progress

into uncharted territory.

Amen.

You are the light of the world...
a lamp...gives light to everyone in the house.

Matthew 5:14–15, NIV

Fathers, Keep Your Lights On

Mark Weinrich

Every fall, with the first chill of frost, animals seek refuge in warm places. One fall evening our family returned home after dark. We hadn't turned on the porch light because we'd expected to return earlier.

I opened the front door and flipped on the light. "What's that?" my wife screamed.

I glanced down as a thirteen-inch rattlesnake slithered off the door sill and through the open door. There was no time to react, no time to slam the door.

What could I do? A rattlesnake can be a disturbing creature anytime, even if he's a small one. But what happens when he invites himself into your home?

I edged the door farther open and peeked inside. The rattler coiled and buzzed. What volume! The snake's warning magnified, echoing in the confines of the entryway.

The rattlesnake captured my attention, backing and buzzing his way under the dark space of the entry area closet door. There's not much on that closet floor, so I could imagine the snake crawling into the vacuum cleaner. My son slid behind me and ran into the kitchen. I yelled, "Matt, bring me the broom."

Broom in hand, I jerked the door open and swept the snake into the hall. Then I opened the front door, swept the furious rattler onto the porch, and pinned him with the broom. Matt brought the garden hoe and I dispatched the intruder.

Later I meditated on the ordeal and realized the snake hadn't invited himself in. I had let him in! If I'd left the porch light on, he'd have found another warm, dark place to sleep. I, the father, the head of the household, had let the serpent in!

I wondered, had I let other harmful things enter our home? What a startling question, as startling as the rattler's buzz! It didn't matter whether it was intentional or not. Had I introduced or allowed harmful things in our home?

Christian fathers should be the light of their families, just as Christ is to them. Does my devotional life with the Lord have the intensity to guide, help, and protect my family through their physical and spiritual growth?

The rattlesnake incident caused me to reevaluate my time in prayer and in God's Word. By God's grace and wisdom, my light is shining a little better now. And the porch light is shining, too, one great sweep of light, chasing darkness and intruders from our path and our home.

Father,
let Your Word and Spirit illuminate my life
that my light may lead others to You.
Amen.

Sir, give me this water,
so I will not be thirsty nor come all the way here to draw.

John 4:15, NASB

An Old Piece of Pipe

Donald E. White

I have usually found northwestern Canada in the summer to be a land of breathtaking beauty, with snow-capped mountains, beautiful rivers and lakes, evergreen forests, wilderness meadows, and a pleasant, cool climate. However, one family trip back to Alaska did not meet with such expectations.

I remember that trip very well. It was hot, dusty, and quite miserable. The temperature was near a record high. The sun was intense; the air, still. The lack of rain and the vehicle traffic had made the gravel of the old Alaska highway a dust bowl. With our car windows up, the heat was unbearable, and with them down, we choked on the dust.

I couldn't imagine discomfort being worse for the children, but then voices from the backseat informed me they were out of drinking water. I tried to console the children in their misery, but without much success.

There was excitement a few miles later when a simple, hand-painted sign appeared by the roadside. It read, "Spring Water Ahead." We ran to the spring, drank our fill, washed our faces, and filled water bottles. We talked with other travelers about the refreshment of the cool, clear water on such a hot day. Words could not adequately express our gratitude.

Then I saw it, the pipe! It was just an old piece of pipe, bent and dusty, protruding from a crevice in the rocks. Yes, it was just a piece of pipe, but it was much more; it was the conduit providing us with precious spring water that quenched our thirst and brought relief in time of need.

Children and adults alike would take hold of the old pipe, lean over and drink. I noticed that many adjectives were used to extol the qualities of the spring water, but no one mentioned the pipe. The truly thirsty focused on the cool, thirst-quenching water, not on the conduit!

As we continued our journey, I thought about that old piece of pipe and about how we as Christians are conduits to carry God's gift to those who thirst for the rivers of Living Water. Imperfect as we are, it's comforting to know that God wants to use us and that His love and grace overshadow our weaknesses.

Dear Lord,
thank You for the one who carried
the Living Water of Your Son, Jesus Christ to me.
Please help me to convey Your love and grace to others.
Amen.

And let us not lose heart in doing good,
for in due time we shall reap if we do not grow weary.

Galatians 6:9, NASB

Some Seeds Grow Slowly

Gene Wilder

Each Sunday morning, before worship begins, I enjoy chatting with those who arrive early. I receive a variety of responses from those I greet. Some just shake my hand and say, "Good morning, Pastor," while others take the time to engage in more lengthy conversations.

One little girl is always a challenge to me. Despite my most valiant efforts, I never get a spoken response from her. Sometimes she gives me a cute little grin, sometimes a handshake, but never a spoken word.

I often wondered what went on in her mind as I approached. Was she frightened of me? Did she think I was just another one of those nosy adults?

Regardless of the reason for her silence, something in her shy little smile compelled me to speak to her week after week. Some hidden charm drew me to her despite the continued absence of her oral reply.

Then one Sunday, my cute little friend handed me a flower and a folded note as she left the sanctuary. Again, no word was uttered, although her smile seemed a little bigger than usual. After she left, I looked at the note that accompanied the big red iris. In elementary scrawl and spelling, the note read:

This is love.
Thanks for evarthing.
You talked to me.

I kept the iris on my desk all week long. And, while flowers seldom speak, this bloom said more than words could ever utter.

At times, all of us wonder if we're getting through to those around us. We talk, but we hear no reply. We smile, but often receive only stares. We hug, but no one hugs back. We try to impact the lives of others, but we wonder if others even notice. We sow the seeds of love, only to reap a harvest of famine.

Sometimes the love we sow finds fertile ground. Sometimes, from ground that previously seemed barren, shoots forth the bud of compassion's life. Sometimes the shy little smile of a quiet girl blossoms into the full flower of an appreciative response.

Love's seeds don't always grow as soon as they're sown, but when they do, the beauty of the flower is worth the effort of the planting and patient nurturing.

Dear Lord,
nothing is more difficult than sowing love in unresponsive soil. Give
me the endurance to continue planting
and the faith to wait for love's blossoms to appear.
In Jesus' name I pray.
Amen.

And be kind to one another, tender-hearted, forgiving each other,
just as God in Christ has also forgiven you.

Ephesians 4:32, NASB

How Do We Learn Affection?

Ed Young

Men do things every day that are "not our nature." It is not my nature to sit in meetings for several hours, but there are times that I do so. It is not my nature to be sweet and affectionate, either, but with practice I can make it a habit.

I remember walking through the den one day and seeing my wife, JoBeth, scratch our dog Sonny's back. She rubbed Sonny's back and he was just so content that I said, "You know, I wish you'd rub my back like that." She didn't miss a beat. She said, "If you were as sweet as Sonny, I would!" So I'm working on it.

Some of you men may be thinking you are at a loss when it comes to showing the woman you married affection. Maybe you are not sure what really satisfies her desire in this area. I have a revolutionary suggestion: Ask her! You are married to the best teacher in the world. Wives are "Phi Beta Kappa" in affection. They know what to do.

JoBeth writes little notes for me when I travel. She is thoughtful about this, interested in that, and on and on. She knows how to express affection. And if I ask her, she can readily describe the kind of affection she'd like to receive from me. When men do that, the mystery is solved. They are without excuse.

My good friend Cliff Barrows says that there are twelve words that can breathe life into any relationship: *I am sorry. I was wrong. Please forgive me. I love you.* These are the words of tenderhearted kindness and affection, and the one who remembers and uses them will soon come to understand their power to change the hardest of hearts and the most hopeless of circumstances.

Father,

I pray You will teach me to be tender, teach me to be loving,

teach me to be forgiving, teach me to be more like You.

I know, dear Lord,

You want me to be as deliberate and careful with my relationships

as You are with Yours.

And I'm forever grateful that You are patient in Your teaching.

Amen.

And be kind to one another, tender-hearted, forgiving each other,

just as God in Christ has also forgiven you.

Ephesians 4:32, NASB

Men Friends

Don M. Aycock

I had many friends when I was growing up, but one was special. His name was Milton. As boys, Milton and I were almost inseparable. We lived a half-mile apart in a rural area of Louisiana.

In our area there were woods, swamps, pastures, a bayou, and we knew every square inch of them. Together Milton and I hunted, fished, went to school, and played basketball and softball. In the pastures we even threw cow muffins at each other.

We swung from vines over Bayou Des Canes, giving our Tarzan yells as we let go of the vines and hit the water. We climbed small pine saplings, grabbed the tops, and jumped out so the trees would bend and give us an elevator ride down. Sometimes the tops would snap off and our ride down would be faster than we wanted! It was all great fun.

Milton and I would pick mayhaws in the swamps and ride around in homemade boats during flood times. He had a huge abandoned sawdust pile behind his house, and we spent many hours tunneling through it with old stockings over our heads to keep the sawdust out of our eyes and noses. We were friends and would do anything with or for each other.

Milton and I don't see each other very often now. We've gone our separate ways. But I still hold him in high esteem. And I cherish the good times we had and their value for me as an adult.

I believe the need for good friends doesn't end with childhood. As an adult, the memory of my friendship with Milton helps me realize the importance of close ties with other men. We're not meant to be loners!

Competition, the drive for success, and the daily demands of our family and professional lives often seem to drive a wedge between men. Many of us don't take the time to make and keep good, intimate friends. But that wedge should be thrown out.

Give some thought today to your friends and, while you are, thank God for them.

Lord,

thanks for my childhood friends

who were both adventurous and foolish with me.

They helped me grow into the man I am today.

And thank You for the friends I have now.

They really are friends who stick closer than brothers.

Amen.

Grandchildren are the crown of the aged.

Proverbs 17:6, NRSV

When Generations Meet

William H. Gentz

Now that I have reached the age of grandparenting, I know personally the truth of these words from Proverbs. My grandchildren have a special place in my heart, and even though they do not live close by, any contact with them is precious. Anyone who cares for the aged should be especially aware of this fact.

Some of the most meaningful memories of my childhood include my grandparents. Since I was a child of parents who were the oldest in their families, I had the privilege of knowing my grandparents until I was grown.

One of my fondest memories is that of my grandfather on my father's side. In his last days he reverted to speaking German, the language of his youth. But he had done so well integrating his family into their new American home and language that by this time his children had forgotten what German they had known. So they could not be of much help, especially in Grandfather's devotional and spiritual life, which had deep roots in another tongue.

This is where I came into the picture and saw a side of my grandfather that I had never known. When I was small I was curious about the language he spoke to my grandmother and the words in the funny script he read in his newspaper. The words that he sang while at work in his carpenter shop intrigued me. It was from Grandfather that I learned my first bits of German, which, in turn, sparked my interest to study the language in both high school and college. By the time he was in his last years, I had enough skill to be able to answer my aunt's call for help to come and read to Grandfather from the Bible and pray with him in his native tongue.

As I read his favorite passages from Scripture and prayed the *Vater unser* with him, I saw a light in his eyes that was more brilliant than I had ever seen there before. My grandfather also taught me to appreciate his favorite hymn, "So nimm denn meine Hande" (O Take My Hand and Lead Me) with its clear message of our dependence on our heavenly Father and the necessity to put our hands in His through life and into eternity.

As a young person, I prayed hard that I could be God's messenger in that difficult situation, but now I thank God for this blessing of learning to know my grandfather's faith. Hopefully, for him, I was the crown of his old age.

Thank You, Lord,
for the privilege of sharing my faith in Christ
between the generations.
Amen.

He looked up and said,
"I see people; they look like trees walking around."

Mark 8:24, NIV

Presbyopia

Robert S. Hampel

The first time I saw the word, or the first time it registered with me, was about thirty years ago. I was in a waiting room of an optometrist's office. A row of pamphlets caught my attention. They had been prepared to explain diseases of the eye. One of them was titled "Presbyopia."

I picked up the pamphlet and read it, and I remember thinking at the time that anything that sounded that much like Presbyterian should be looked into. As a young Presbyterian minister, I reacted inside to the idea that *presby* would be associated with a disease—or optic problem.

As I read through the article about presbyopia, I realized that I, indeed, had it. Presbyopia is the loss of ability to focus adequately on objects that are near to us. It means having to use eyeglasses for close reading, or else holding what we're reading farther from us. In other words, those of us with presbyopia have difficulty seeing things close up. I checked the word in the dictionary, too. It says, "a defect of vision associated with old age." *Presby* is Greek for "old man." And *opia* refers to the eyes.

I've decided that presbyopia is not only a physical problem, it's a spiritual problem as well.

The eighth chapter of Mark tells of a time when Jesus gave sight to a man who was blind. One of the most interesting aspects of this healing is that the man was healed in stages, not all at once. After Jesus had first used saliva and touched the man's eyes, He asked him, "Do you see anything?" The man answered, "I see people; they look like trees walking around." Then Jesus laid His hands on the man's eyes again and he saw everything clearly.

Our Lord has opened our eyes spiritually. But we have need to ask Him to open the eyes of our minds and hearts more. We need His touch, that we might see things in perspective. We need to see people with clarity—and with charity. We need to see persons, not as objects to be manipulated or as trees walking around. We need to see them as persons precious in God's sight.

Dear God,
help me to see people as You see them,
that I might love them as You do.
In Jesus' name.
Amen.

A person's words can be a source of wisdom,
deep as the ocean, fresh as a flowing stream.

Proverbs 18:4, TEV

The Gift of Conversation

James H. Harrison

Meeting friends for coffee and conversation is one of life's privileges. A group of us who shared this mutual affection met twice a week. One of the group, Swede, had a reputation for being rude, overbearing, and forceful. These attributes, along with his large size and position of authority, earned him the reputation of an intimidating bully. I was not affected by his circle of influence, so regardless of his reputation, I found him interesting and enjoyed our conversations.

Early one morning, Swede came to my office and asked if we could talk. I could tell by the look on his face that this wasn't going to be one of our normal conversations. "I've got a problem," he said. "I haven't been sleeping; it just keeps going around in my head. When the lights are out, I panic."

So began the story of his childhood abuses. He didn't know his father. His mother entertained men, and when she did she locked Swede in dark, musty closets. If he made any noise she would "beat manners into him" when the men left.

He likened the experience to being buried alive. The closet was his casket. As the story continued, Swede opened up all of the old fears and angers that lay recessed in the folds and fissures of his memory. Anger and fear had ruined his three marriages, his ability to parent, and his skills to communicate with others.

Over the next two years, Swede and I had many conversations. We talked about moving beyond fears and anger that controlled us and how to determine when they were taking over. But most importantly, we discussed God's forgiving grace and how the compassion from Jesus' ministry would proclaim him healed.

Our intimate conversations changed both of our lives. Swede's position of authority became a stepping-stone to help others create a motivated workplace, and I gained a genuine friend for life.

Heavenly Father,
may You always be the center of every friendship
as I communicate the pain in my life
and turn my fears and angers into wisdom.
In Jesus' name.
Amen.

Yet I hold this against you:
You have forsaken your first love.

Revelation 2:4, NIV

The Honeymoon Is Over!

Louis Merryman

I knew our honeymoon was over when my bride of six months no longer got up with me before the crack of dawn on the Saturdays and Sundays when I was in the Air National Guard. In our first months together I would get ready for my duty as a weekend warrior while she fixed us a beautiful breakfast. Then she'd join me as I scarfed mine down. Only after I left to go to the nearby Air Force Base, did she make her way back to slumberland.

Breakfast had also played a significant part of our courtship. On my way to work before we were married, I would pick up doughnuts and drop by the doctor's office she opened early every morning. We'd dunk doughnuts and stare into each other's eyes until I had to leave. First love.

The damage to our honeymoon occurred during an Officers' Dining Out. That's when the officers of a military unit and their sweethearts get together for a dinner-dance. The other wives were most energetic in putting down my bride's early morning cooking habits. They said she was setting a bad example for the rest of them. So she stopped.

One of the benchmarks of a first love is the desire to be together. Similarly, many new Christians are known for spending every moment they can in worship, prayer, Bible study, and sharing their newfound love with their friends. From dawn to dusk they want to be with their first love.

In the letter sent to the church at Ephesus, Jesus commended them for their deeds, their hard work, and their perseverance. However, they were condemned for having lost their first love. Now this was a heavy accusation, for this was not just any church.

This was the church where the apostle John, the one who was called the beloved disciple, was known as one of the leaders. Corporately, the church at Ephesus had forsaken its first love.

How do we keep things cooking in our relationship with Jesus—and with our brides? How do we find our first love again? Jesus doesn't leave us starving for the answer. It's found in Revelation 2:5: "Repent and do the things you did at first."

Lord Jesus,
help me to love You today as I did when I first loved You.
Help me to love my wife in the same way.
Amen.

His mother called his name Jabez, saying,
"Because I bore him in pain."
And Jabez called on the God of Israel saying,
"Oh, that You would bless me...that I may not cause pain!"
So God granted him what he requested.

Chronicles 4:9–10, NKJV

No More Pain!

Lester W. Smith

A man I'll call John came to me a few years ago for pastoral counseling. His wife had insisted he come because of how demanding he was of their son.

John admitted that his boy was a compliant teenager. He also confessed he had rather unrealistic expectations which his son was unable to meet. I found John was willing to explore the reasons for the breakdown in his relationship with his son.

As we talked over the next few weeks, I discovered that John hadn't visited his own parents for ten years. The problem in their relationship went back to his childhood and unresolved conflict. You see, John was born with a cleft palate, and his parents constantly reminded him that he was "different." His father refused to allow him to play sports or engage in activities like the so-called "normal kids." Instead, John was held to very rigid standards working around their home.

I suggested some appropriate Scriptures that John could apply to alter his behavior toward his son. Basically, he was practicing the role of parenting he had learned from his own parents. Unfortunately, he was repeating the misguided treatment he had received from his own father. I also encouraged John to be reconciled with his parents. We prayed together for God's grace to forgive them.

As it turned out, John's dad died a short time later. John was able to speak to him briefly just before his death. The funeral also opened the door for reconciliation with his mother. John was finally able to release his pain, and the result was positive change in his relationship with his son.

Every Christmas I get an envelope from John with two hundred dollars and a note that it be used to buy toys for poor children in our church and that the contributor must remain anonymous. The note also expresses John's gratitude for God's blessings. His hope is that his Christmas gift will help ease the pain of children in unfortunate circumstances.

John cried out to God and He granted his request, just like Jabez!

Father,
help me to have the same loving approach
with my children that You have with me.
Amen.

As for the saints who are in the earth, they are the majestic ones in whom is all my delight.

Psalm 16:3, NASB

Majestic Ones

Mark Weinrich

When I was a senior in Bible college I became ill just before my six-week exams. I was married, working part-time, and taking a heavy course load. I had no time for illness.

My sickness kept me bedfast for weeks. During that time I worried because I knew I was getting farther behind in my studies. When I finally returned to class I despaired of ever catching up. I went to my advisor with the intent of dropping out and coming back the next year. He, however, encouraged me not to drop out. In fact, he'd talked to all of my professors and made arrangements for me to make up the work.

With my advisor's help and the encouragement of many friends, I finished the last makeup assignment on the last day of finals and graduated on time.

I look back at how my friends and professors supported me in staying faithful to the Lord's course. If they hadn't stood by me I'd probably have dropped out. Those friends and professors are the "majestic ones" to me. They are godly men who stood beside me through a difficult time.

King David became the man of God he was partly because of the godly men he had around him. Through much of his life he was a man on the run, a man finding trouble at every turn, yet God placed "majestic ones" in his life to support him and help him remain faithful.

God has placed many "majestic ones" in my life and I delight in them. I'm thankful for those brothers in the Lord who have stood beside me and helped me become what God desires me to be. Without them, who knows how I would have turned out.

Father,

thank You for the "majestic ones" You have placed in my life.

May I be a "majestic one" to others and help them grow in You.

Amen.

God made...all the creatures that move along the ground according to their kinds. And God saw that it was good.

Genesis 1:25, NIV

The Cleanest Snake in Town

W. Peter West

"Help! Come quickly!" she yelled from the basement. My wife's scream interrupted a leisurely Saturday morning.

Our two young boys joined me in responding to my wife's plea. We found her peering inside of the washing machine.

"It's in there!" she gasped.

My youngest son, David, was the first to look inside the washer. "Dad, it's a snake! A real live snake!"

This was a problem I had never tackled before. Besides, I had a terrible fear of snakes. But the problem would not go away. It had to be solved.

After a quick prayer for guidance I saw two pieces of wood on the floor, part of the "junk" our sons always seem to bring into the house.

Taking the pieces of wood, I gingerly reached forward, cradled the hissing snake in the "V," and proceeded slowly up the stairs with the snake dangling from the sticks. At a suitable distance my wife and children followed. We all hoped it wouldn't fall off.

Beneath the rear window, just a few steps away from the house, we have a small, poorly maintained flower garden. With my arms stretched to full length in front of me, and with the snake beginning to wriggle and slide off, I placed him carefully amongst the flowers and weeds. The snake slowly raised its head, took a last look at us, and glided away into the underbrush. As it disappeared, we decided none of its markings looked as if it were one of the poisonous varieties.

We never did find out how the snake got into our washing machine, but as one of my boys remarked rather wryly, "Dad, it was the cleanest snake in town!" Ironically, his observation was most accurate.

Most of us rank snakes with some disdain, in part, due to their scriptural reputation. A lot more of us justifiably fear them because of the real danger some of them represent. Yet, as much as I'm afraid of snakes, I must admit, aside from causing a little more commotion in our home, that snake had done us no harm. It was "clean," and not any more deserving of prejudgment than any other of His creations. Snakes surely have their place in God's plan, as we all do.

O Lord,

help me to respect all creatures great and small,

even the creepy, crawly ones that make me afraid.

Amen.

But the Lord said to Samuel,
"Do not look on his appearance or on the height of his stature...
for the Lord does not see as mortals see;
they look on the outward appearance,
but the Lord looks on the heart.

1 Samuel 16:7, NRSV

The Not-So-Incredible Hulk

Gene Wilder

Last summer my wife and I flew from Atlanta to Baltimore. As we boarded the plane we were startled by the loud, husky voices of a dozen or more gigantic men boarding behind us. Not one of them was shorter than six-and-a-half feet. Their ragged T-shirts and cut-off jeans made them look even more conspicuous than their gargantuan size.

One of the hulks sat in front of us, one sat behind us, and another sat across the aisle from us. For the most part, these characters were loud and rude. Each would have profited greatly from a lesson in appropriate plane courtesy. Ironically, no one questioned their unusual behavior. I guess when you're nearly seven feet tall and weigh 375 pounds few people question anything you do.

My wife recognized them before I did. "Aren't those guys professional wrestlers?" she asked.

"Honey," I replied. "Those guys are more than just wrestlers. Those guys are bona fide *wrasslers.*" Our suspicions were later confirmed as I saw one of them studying a World Championship Wrestling itinerary.

Just before our plane landed, one of the "wrasslers" pulled a small photo album from his travel bag. As he carefully opened the cover, I saw a picture of this giant man tenderly holding a newborn. Obviously, he was a new father. He spent several minutes just gazing at the pictures, and as he did his cold, hard face began to soften with the ache of loneliness.

Suddenly, it dawned on me. He and I were not so different after all. Despite the obvious external differences, both of us had the same internal need. Both of us found our deepest fulfillment in the tenderness of somebody's love.

As we make our way through life, most of us tend to evaluate people by what we see on the outside. Such evaluations always accentuate the obvious differences.

The Bible tells us that God sees man not from the outside, but from the inside. Through God's eyes all of us look the same. God sees past the hulk and bulk of our worldly shells to the tender places of our hearts. Wouldn't this world be a better place if we could do the same?

Dear Lord,

give me eyes to see others as You see them;

not from the hulk and bulk of their external veneer

but from the warm and tender depths of their hearts.

In Jesus' name I pray.

Amen.

A man of many companions may come to ruin,
but there is a friend who sticks closer than a brother.

Proverbs 18:24, NIV

Friendships

Charles R. Brown

In an old box of grade school photographs, I found a black-and-white picture of me with a boy named Billy. We were neighbors in Illinois. In the photo, we're standing with our arms around each other's neck, our wide eyes filled with the simple fun of being together.

When my family lived in St. Louis I'd go over to my fourth grade friend Steve's house and play. While living in Indiana, I spent many days with my junior high basketball buddy, Hank. In college I roomed with Denis, with whom I exchanged many life-changing thoughts. It was in college, too, that my friend Ron carried me into the hospital one time. Two of my best friends have been my brothers, Max and Bob.

Early in 1974 I met Chuck. Since then I've been blessed with a taste of the relationship David and Jonathan must have had as it's described in the book of First Samuel. We're one in spirit, and each of us loves the other as himself. We've served together in ministry. Our families have often played together. We've had the joy of giving gifts and celebrating special days.

We've studied and prayed together. God has taught me much as this friend has opened the Word and opened his life to me. The practical application of God's principles became flesh; relationships took on new meaning; finances made sense for the first time in my life.

A great part of the glue that's kept us together revolves around his demonstration of his love for Christ. My friend, Chuck, accepts me no matter what my circumstances or state of mind. He has the freedom to shape me up, but he has never told me to ship out! Even when I fail he remains my friend. When I disappoint him he loves me anyway. When he's aware of sin in my life, he gently, without arrogance, leads me to that holy place where God can do His work. We're friends and there are no strings attached. Well, that's not completely accurate. There *are* strings attached. Those strings form cords of love, acceptance, and accountability.

I place special value on all the close friendships I've had over the years. In this day of superficial relationships I feel richly blessed with this particular friendship. God has blessed me with someone who is willing to give counsel. He has given me a sounding board off which I can bounce ideas, whether they be serious or ridiculous. Chuck is a fellow traveler that is deeply concerned with my spiritual well-being. He gives without any expectation of receiving anything in return. May we all give of ourselves freely and be blessed with such endearing friendships.

Father in heaven,
make me the kind of friend that the Lord Jesus was
when He walked among men—
giving, caring, listening, teaching.
In His name I pray.
Amen.

Give an account of your stewardship.

Luke 16:2, NASB

Stewardship

Robert Busha

Mention *stewardship* and my thoughts naturally go first to money and how it's handled or how a business account is managed. But with even modest reflection I know I have a much greater area of responsibility. Yes, there's personal, family, and business finances and possessions which are obviously under my care. That's easy to tally. However, with serious reflection, my list of accounts gets even longer.

The health of my mind and body, spiritually and physically, are near the top, too. And there's the health of those around me—family, friends, acquaintances. To some degree they're my concern as well. And there's the financial and organizational health of our church. That's assigned to me, along with the other members of the congregation who are my family, too. I believe God demands I minister to them as best I can.

Thinking about it a little more and then looking around me, my ledger of accounts seems to be much larger than I may have wanted to admit. There's our community and every level of our government and public properties and the environment and…well, there's so much more

I sometimes prefer to ignore or take for granted. Most of it seems beyond my personal influence, but I know it's part of my stewardship nonetheless. I've thought about protesting: "I'm just one guy. How can I possibly take care of everything?" Actually, I know the answer, and it's a rather simple concept called *sharing*.

In every dimension of my stewardship, I can look to my Christian brothers of like mind for help. Where I'm not strong or not aware or not close at hand, I can encourage and pray for others who are willing and able to share in watching over the accounts we share. I realize now, even with sharing, I can't slide by my accounts anymore.

For me, this is the final and most compelling thought which summarizes the devotions in this book. As in the parable of the unrighteous steward in the gospel of Luke, I'm certain I'll be held accountable. I won't be able to plead ignorance. I won't be permitted to deny responsibility. I won't be allowed to slip away from the ultimate assessment He will make of me. If I'm aware and if I'm able, I'll be held accountable for all that I can, and should, do.

Father,

I want to take better care of the accounts You have assigned to me.

I relinquish myself to You and to my brothers

to be accountable for my responsibilities.

Thank You for all You have provided

and will continue to provide.

Amen.

Meet Our Contributors

Don M. Aycock loves the outdoors, traveling, and writing. He is author of many articles and books including *God's Most Unmistakable Message, Eight Days That Changed the World, Walking Straight in a Crooked World, Apathy in the Pew, and Inside Religious Publishing.* Don and his wife, Carla, have twin boys and make their home in Lake Charles, Louisiana. He is the president of the Louisiana Christian Writers' Guild.

Harold Behm is a retired electrical engineer. He and his wife, Mary Jane, live in Charlotte, North Carolina. They have three grown daughters, each living in another state. His interests include writing, computers, photography, and woodworking.

Charles Brown works for a title insurance company, is an elder in his church and is worship leader. He and his wife, Bobbie, have four children and live in Riverside, California. Charles is a charter member of the Inland Empire Writers' Guild.

Bob Busha focuses on leadership for individual and organizational development, especially in the church. He and his wife, Mary Catherine, live and work in Santa Rosa, California. Their life is almost totally consumed by helping bring books to life. Bob loves the mountains, the ocean, and hiking and backpacking in remote places.

John Calsin lives in West Chester, Pennsylvania. He is a free-lance writer, newspaper columnist, essayist, and editorialist, "who works temporary jobs periodically to keep from starving." He is a member of the Greater Philadelphia Christian Writers' Fellowship, and is a Sunday School teacher. He is recently married to Carol and loves it.

Jerry Cook is the assistant pastor at Eastside Foursquare Church in Kirkland, Washington. He is author of *A Few Things I've Learned Since I Knew It All,* co-author with his wife, Barbara, of the book *How to Raise Good Kids,* and with Stanley Baldwin of *Love, Acceptance, and Forgiveness.*

Jack Cunningham is a freelance writer based in Kenner, Louisiana. His work has appeared in *Young Salvationist, Christian Single, Vital Christianity, The Advocate, The Upper Room, Light from the Word,* and other publications. Jack's spare-time activities include golfing, fishing, and reading history.

Dean Davis is a youth pastor and a pro-life organization staff member. Dean and his wife, Linda, and their five children live in Santa Rosa, California.

James Dobson is founder and president of Focus on the Family. He and his wife, Shirley, parents of two grown children, live in Colorado Springs, Colorado. He is the author of *When God Doesn't Make Sense, The New Dare to Discipline, Straight Talk to Men and Their Wives, Love Must Be Tough,* and *Love for a Lifetime.*

Phil Downer is president of the Christian Business Men's Committee of the USA. He and his wife, Susy, and their six children live in Chattanooga, Tennessee.

Bernie Epperson is the shipping and receiving supervisor for a company in Oneida, New York. He enjoys writing, drama, gardening, softball, and working with teens. Bernie performs Christian satirical sketches for church and community groups.

Mark Evans is a staff writer and columnist for the *Press Leader* newspaper in Farmington, Missouri. He has served as sports editor in

Dexter and Kennett, Missouri. He is associate youth minister at First Baptist Church of Bonne Terre and helps teach youth Sunday School.

Bill Gentz has edited or written six books and many magazine articles. He is a Lutheran clergyman who has served over the years in four states. Most of his career has been as a book editor for several publishers. He teaches writing for the Christian marketplace at the New York School of the Bible. Bill resides in New York City.

Bob Hampel is a retired pastor, now serving part-time as a minister of visitation for a church in Healdsburg, California. He and his wife, Carolyn, reside in Santa Rosa.

James Harrison lives in Rancho Cordova, California. He is president of the Sacramento Christian Writers' Club, and he records taped books for the learning disabled and blind. Jim has taught in elementary school and served as pastor in United Methodist churches in Nevada and California.

David Hauk is an optometrist in group practice and lives in Reading, Pennsylvania, with his wife, Debra, and their three children. In addition to collecting foreign and ancient coins, and getting more serious about his writing, the majority of Dave's free time is taken up with his family . . . and he loves it.

R. Kent Hughes is senior pastor of College Church in Wheaton, Illinois. He is a prolific author, and he and his wife, Barbara, have four children. He has written *Disciplines of Grace, Disciplines of a Godly Man, Abba Father: The Lord's Pattern for Prayer, Living on the Cutting Edge,* and *Liberating Ministry from the Success Syndrome.*

Chris Johnson is a technical sales representative for an environmental management company. He and his wife, Teresa, live in Lexington, Kentucky. Chris loves all sports, and received the Presidential Sports Award in 1991.

Max Lucado is heard weekly on the national radio program, "UpWords." His many books include *God Came Near, And the Angels Were Silent, No Wonder They Call Him the Savior,* and *Six Hours One Friday.* He and his wife, Denalyn, live in San Antonio, Texas. They have three daughters. Max preaches at the Oak Hills Church of Christ.

Michael Martin and his wife and two teenage boys live in Fairfax, Virginia. He enjoys running, hiking, nature, and sports, and working for environmental organizations. Mike is a lawyer and new writer. His work has been published in *The Upper Room.*

Josh McDowell is an author and speaker. Besides representing Campus Crusade for Christ, he heads Josh McDowell Ministries. The McDowells have four children and reside in California. He is the author of twenty-eight books, including *Evidence That Demands a Verdict, More Than a Carpenter,* and *Evidence of Joy.*

Lt. Col. Louis Merryman (USAFR, Ret.) loves to watch movies and to write plays, devotionals, and other articles, many of which have been published and performed. His latest play is *Ernie and the Christmas Angels.* He also likes hot air ballooning. Louis lives in El Segundo, California.

Dennis Meyers lives in Camarillo, California, with his wife, Barbara. He's an administrator with GTE California, a licensed private pilot, and loves "reading, bicycling, gardening, walking, and the Lord with all my heart."

Patrick Morley is founder and president of Morley Properties, Inc., which acquires and develops office, retail, and industrial properties. He resides with his family in central Florida. He is the author of *The Man in the Mirror: Solving the 24 Problems Men Face.*

Al Munger and his wife live in Poulsbo, Washington. He retired a few years ago after pastoring for thirty-two years. Al has written for *Viewpoint* magazine. He enjoys RV travel, photography, woodworking, and radio-controlled airplanes. Al is pastor-in-residence at Northwest College in Kirkland.

Gerry Presley is the worship leader and an elder with Grace Fellowship Church in Santa Rosa, California. In business, he is the used car sales manager for a large car dealership in the city. Gerry and his wife, Aurora, have three children, Jennifer, Jason, and Jonathon.

Jason Presley is a senior English major at Pepperdine University in Malibu, California. His hobbies include making greeting cards; playing guitar, harmonica, and percussion instruments; and writing songs, poetry, fiction, and children's literature. He edits *Expressionists,* Pepperdine's literary and arts magazine.

Brad Sargent likes operatic whistling, puns, making people laugh, and hunting for out-of-print books. He lives in San Rafael, California, and is director of research for Exodus International, a worldwide network of Christian ministries. Brad serves on the Board of Directors of Christian AIDS Services Alliance.

Scott Sibley lives in King of Prussia, Pennsylvania, with his wife, Carol, and their three children. He is a professional engineer specializing in transportation projects including railroads, highways, and bus facilities. His hobbies are bicycling and home improvement projects. Scott is an elder in the First Presbyterian Church of Bridgeport, Pennsylvania.

Mike Slater is married and the father of two children. He is pastor of Temple Baptist Church in LaHabra, California. Mike is the author of the book *Becoming a Stretcher Bearer: Lifting One Another in Times of Need with the Gifts of Encouragement and Support.*

Gary Smalley teaches seminars throughout North America on marriage and the family. Among his many books are *If Only He Knew, For Better or for Best, The Joy of Committed Love, Joy That Lasts,* and with Dr. John Trent *Love Is a Decision, The Blessing,* and *The Language of Love.* Gary is founder and president of Today's Family.

Les Smith is senior pastor of Richfield Road United Brethren in Christ Church in Flint, Michigan. He and his wife, Linda, have two children. Les has memorized and performs, in costume, twelve New Testament books. He has given presentations throughout America, in two foreign countries, and on Christian television.

Robert Smith is pastor of Calvary Baptist Church in Compton, California. He has written numerous magazine articles and has recently contracted with the National Baptist Convention to publish his book *The Hebrew Names for God,* and with Baker Books for his book *Blacks and Cults.* He and his wife, Margaret, live in Pasadena. Robert loves church league basketball, reading, and writing.

Russell Spray is a retired pastor who with his wife, Pauline, lives in Lapeer, Michigan. They have two daughters, five granddaughters, and one great-grandson. Russell is the author of twenty-three sermon outline books.

John Strubhar is senior pastor at Brookside Church of Fort Wayne, Indiana. He has written numerous magazine articles, and co-authored *Evangelistic Preaching: A Step by Step Guide to Pulpit Evangelism.* He and his wife, Sandra, have three daughters. John's pastimes include golf, tennis, and reading.

Chuck Swindoll is pastor of First Evangelical Free Church in Fullerton, California, and President of the Dallas Theological Seminary in Texas. Chuck and his wife, Cynthia, have four adult children. He has written more than twenty best-selling books including *The Quest for Character, Flying Closer to the Flame: A Passion for the Holy Spirit,* and *Come Before Winter and Share My Hope.*

Fred Van Nice is a supervisor in database administration in Racine, Wisconsin. Fred is the father of three and is currently engaged to a wonderful Christian woman. He sings in his church choir, plays the guitar, and likes woodworking.

Stu Weber and his wife, Linda, partnered together in the founding of Good Shepherd Church in Oregon, where he pastors. They speak together at Family Life marriage and parenting conferences across the nation. The Webers have three grown sons. Stu is the author of the book *Tender Warrior: God's Intention for Man.*

Vern Wedeven lives in Newtown Square, Pennsylvania, with his wife, Carol. They have four grown children. Vern is a widely published tribologist and is president of his own company, which specializes in testing and research for ball bearings and lubricants. Vern loves sports, especially tennis, racquetball, basketball, and skiing.

Mark Weinrich is a Christian and Missionary Alliance pastor in Truth or Consequences, New Mexico. Over 280 of his poems, short stories, and articles have been accepted for publication. Four of his early reader books and three juvenile mysteries are soon to be released. When he's not writing, Mark likes hiking, collecting Indian artifacts, exploring caves, and backpacking.

Peter West and his wife, Vera, live in Golden Valley, Minnesota. He is pastor emeritus of First Baptist Church in Minneapolis. Peter enjoys photography and fishing and serving as a board member on the Greater Minneapolis Association of Evangelicals. He is the author of the book *Men of Faith* and has written articles appearing in *Decision* magazine.

Don White is a semi-retired pastor and missionary who spends much of his time writing technical manuals for Christian schools, traveling, and doing yard work. He and his wife, Ellen, live in Hillsboro, Ohio. They have four grown children living in Alaska.

Gene Wilder is pastor of the First Baptist Church in Fitzgerald, Georgia. He and his wife, Patricia, and their two teenage children live in nearby Lizella. In addition to his writing, Gene likes reading, skiing, golfing, and singing, as well as music composition and performance.

Ed Young and his wife, JoBeth, have three sons and two grandchildren. He is the pastor of the Second Baptist Church of Houston, Texas, and the author of *Romancing the Home: How to Have a Marriage That Sizzles, Against All Odds, The Purpose of Suffering,* and *The Winning Talk.* Ed is currently the president of the Southern Baptist Convention.

Credits

The following articles are used by permission of the publishers.

"See the Person, See Christ" by Jerry Cook was adapted from the book *A Few Things I've Learned Since I Knew It All* by Jerry Cook, © 1989, Word, Inc., Dallas, Texas. Used by permission.

"His Encompassing Love" by James Dobson was adapted from the book *When God Doesn't Make Sense* by James Dobson, © 1993 James Dobson, Inc. Used by permission of Tyndale House Publishers, Inc. All rights reserved.

"The Dividends of Fathering" by R. Kent Hughes was adapted from the book *Disciplines of a Godly Man* by R. Kent Hughes, © 1991. Used by permission of Good News Publishers/Crossway Books, 1300 Crescent Street, Wheaton, IL 60187.

"Final Words, Final Acts" by Max Lucado was adapted from the book *No Wonder They Call Him the Savior* by Max Lucado, Multnomah Books, Questar Publishers, © 1986. Used by permission.

"A Special Kind of Love" by Josh McDowell was adapted from the book *More Than a Carpenter* by Josh McDowell, © 1977 by Tyndale House Publishers, Inc. Used by permission. All rights reserved.

"Does Anyone Really Care?" by Patrick M. Morley was adapted from the book *The Man in the Mirror* by Patrick M. Morley, © 1992 Patrick M. Morley, Thomas Nelson, Inc., Nashville, Tennessee. Used by permission.

"Cry for Help" by Michael Slater was adapted from the book *Becoming a Stretcher Bearer* by Michael Slater, © 1989, Regal Books, Ventura, CA 93003. Used by permission.

"Please, Be Tender" by Gary Smalley was adapted from the book *If Only He Knew* by Gary Smalley, © 1979 by Gary T. Smalley. Used by permission of Zondervan Publishing House.

"My Dad" by Charles R. Swindoll was adapted from the book *Come Before Winter . . . And Share My Hope* by Charles R. Swindoll, © 1985 by Charles R. Swindoll. Used by permission of Zondervan Publishing House.

"Tender Warrior" by Stu Weber was adapted from the book *Tender Warrior* by Stu Weber, Multnomah Books, Questar Publishers, © 1993 by Stu Weber. Used by permission.

"How Do We Learn Affection?" by Ed Young was adapted from the book *Romancing the Home* by Ed Young. Nashville: Broadman & Holman Publishers, © 1993 by Broadman & Holman Publishers. All rights reserved.